Great Missionaries
to the Orient

Great Missionaries to the Orient

by

JOHN THEODORE MUELLER

Biography Index Reprint Series

BOOKS FOR LIBRARIES PRESS
FREEPORT, NEW YORK

Copyright 1948 by
Zondervan Publishing House

Reprinted 1972 by arrangement.

Library of Congress Cataloging in Publication Data

Mueller, John Theodore, 1885–
    Great missionaries to the Orient.

    (Biography index reprint series)
    Bibliography: p.
    1. Missions––Asia. 2. Missionaries. I. Title.
BV3150.M8 1972   266'.023'0922 ₍B₎   78-38330
ISBN 0-8369-8125-1

PRINTED IN THE UNITED STATES OF AMERICA
BY
NEW WORLD BOOK MANUFACTURING CO., INC.
HALLANDALE, FLORIDA 33009

Foreword

CHRISTIANS EVERYWHERE, and of all denominations, are aglow with missionary ardor and are eager to do the Lord's will and carry the banner of His precious Gospel to every part of the world. That is witnessed by scores of missionary publications in every land where Christians live. The world is passing through great tribulation, but that means that the Lord's glorious coming is near. He will not fail His promise. Some day Christ will come again in glory!

So there is much work for us to do everywhere— in our home country, in Europe, in Asia, in Africa, but above all, in the Orient. Japan has been brought near to us, not for exploitation, but for salvation. Korea, the miracle land of missions, has with all her social, economic and political problems one primary and paramount problem: the evangelizing of the country in which marvelous works already have been done. There is still much opportunity for Christian mission work in Formosa, where work has just begun. Beyond these border lands are the vast countries that hold millions of unconverted souls. What shall be our answer to the Lord's command: "Go . . . and preach the gospel to every creature"?

If this book will do just a little to make Christians willing to consecrate themselves anew to the great mission cause of Christ, the writer will indeed feel grateful. Yes, dear Lord, bless this book to Thy great glory.

J. THEODORE MUELLER

St. Louis, Mo.

Acknowledgments

A NUMBER OF BOOKS on missions in the Orient have proved themselves of great help to the author. Although these volumes are listed in the Bibliography at the back of the book, he wishes to acknowledge with special appreciation the following: *The Romance of the Gospel,* by C. T. Thrift; *The Progress of World-Wide Missions,* by R. H. Glover; *Great Missionaries,* by C. C. Creagan; *Verbeck of Japan,* by W. E. Griffis; and above all, the excellent scientific studies on missions by K. S. Latourette. By mentioning these names the writer does not mean to slight others, but merely to give honor to those to whom special honor is due.

With deep gratitude the author desires to acknowledge the helpful services of Prof. E. C. Zimmermann of the Concordia Seminary Mission School, of T. W. Engstrom of the Zondervan Publishing House for important suggestions, the Rev. E. J. Saleska, librarian of the Pritzlaff Concordia Seminary Library, and many others. May God richly reward all those who have helped him in writing this volume, and may it redound to His glory and the welfare of His Church in His great world-mission field.

Blessings upon all who love the Lord Jesus Christ and who do what they can to spread His precious Gospel.

J. T. M.

Contents

1

The Land of the Rising Sun

(Japan)

THE COUNTRY AND ITS PEOPLE

IN THIS BOOK of mission studies we are going to speak of the wonderful works of grace which God has wrought in countries that constitute, as it were, the threshold of Asia, and which today are of great interest to all Christians, since these lands more than others, are affected by the world-crisis which is ours at the present time; so with hearts full of prayer and thanksgiving to our precious Lord let us approach the subject, asking Him to make this study a blessing to ourselves and others and to cause it to magnify His Holy Name.

Of the three countries mentioned, Japan is, no doubt, the most important, and so we shall study it first.

Japan is not a large country for it has an area of only about 260,000 square miles if all of its territory is included, or of only about 176,000 square miles if Korea is excluded; or even of only 147,702 square miles if only the direct island possessions are taken into consideration.

But this relatively small country has a population of about 98,000,000, or about 75,000,000, if merely the direct areas are considered. In other words, the population

is altogether out of proportion to the relatively small areas
in which these millions live. Japan, therefore, has one
characteristic in common with all of Asia, of which it
is a part: "There is too little land for its too many
millions."

Japan consists of four main islands: Honshu in the center, with Hokkaido in the north and Shikoku and Kyushu
in the south. To the north also are the Kurile Islands
and Sakhalin, or Karafuto, while to the south are the
Ryukyu Islands. The large island of Formosa, or Taiwan,
Japan received from China in 1895, at the close of its war
with that country. Thus the area of Japan proper is only
a trifle under the area of California. Over Korea it later
established a protectorate, ruling it with an iron hand.
Greater Japan includes also a number of smaller islands,
of which many have a circumference of only about two
miles.

To give the reader a better idea of the length of Japan's
island possessions, we add that its islands form a long
chain more than two thousand miles long, though none
of them is much wider than about one hundred miles.
Placed on the east coast of our country, they would extend from Maine to Cuba, Tokyo, the capital, lying
somewhere off the coast of North Carolina.

Much of Japan's territory is mountainous and volcanic.
The famous snow-capped volcano, Japan's "sacred mountain," Fujiyama, is 12,395 feet high, but has been dormant
since 1770. Many other volcanoes, however, are active,
and together with many earthquakes, which occur in the
island region, they cause much destruction. Tidal waves
also are frequent, and they cause not only much loss of
property but destroy also thousands of lives.

Life in Japan, therefore, is both hard and dangerous.
Nevertheless, Japan is a beautiful country, with much
attractive mountain scenery, many charming waterfalls
and hundreds of health-giving springs.

The climate in the north is rather cold and the snowfall is heavy, whereas to the south it is warm and pleasant, though the summers frequently are hot, so that the people spend long summer vacations in the fine, cool mountain resorts, of which there are many.

The capital of Japan is Tokyo. Other important cities are Kobe, Kyoto, Osaka and Yokohama, which, in general, are clean and modern and pleasant places in which to live.

Japan is rich in natural resources such as coal, copper, gold, zinc, iron, petroleum, silver, sulphur, lead and other minerals, though its industrial activity is so highly developed that its own supplies are inadequate. Agriculture is, perhaps, the chief occupation of the people, who raise rice, cereals, tobacco, tea and fruits, though mining, silk culture, fishing, factory-work and other occupations keep thousands of others busy. The Japanese are not only a very intelligent but also a very skillfull people, and they export cotton, silk, and rayon textiles, small wares, machinery, sardines and other canned foods.

The ancestors of the modern Japanese no doubt came from Northern Asia, Korea and Malaysia. Thus there have entered into the population Manchu, Mongolian and Malayan strains, but today the people form a homogeneous group. In general, they are neat in person and habits, refined in their tastes, quick-witted, willing to learn and the most progressive of all Asiatics. Their filial piety and patriotism are outstanding, their love for home and country, as also for their government, being exceptionally great. On the other hand, they are also unstable and vacillating, and, under the influence of the military class, they in recent years have coveted Asiatic world-dominion.

Japan became a world-power through its decisive victory in the Russo-Japanese war of 1904. Six years later, in 1910, it annexed Korea. In the First World War Japan gained strategic islands in the Pacific Ocean and secured a strong foothold in China. Rapid expansion followed when the military powers gained the ascendancy. In 1931 Japan invaded Manchuria, in 1937, China. On December 7, 1941, with the unexpected attack on Pearl Harbor, Hawaii, Japan began its terrific drive for the conquest of the Pacific islands and lower Asia.

The future of Japan is uncertain. American rule in conquered Japan has been wise and moderate, and has tended to build up a strong democratic sentiment, and this especially against Russian totalitarianism, which is endeavoring tyrannically to continue the military conquests attempted by Japanese militarism. One fact is sure: to the Christian churches, Japan today offers an inviting field for Christian service in preaching to the still predominantly pagan nation the blessed news of salvation in Christ Jesus. Japan needs Christianity, as does the whole world, for its abiding well-being. If Japan is to have peace, it must receive the Prince of Peace.

BITS OF JAPANESE HISTORY

Japanese historians aver that the authentic history of their country dates from the year 600 B.C., but its reliable history begins with the year 450 A.D. For a long time, it seems, the various islands were held by different tribes, which were independent and often at war with one another. It was only after many years of warfare that these heterogeneous clans were brought under the rule of one supreme head. No doubt Buddhist priests, coming from the Asiatic mainland, brought Chinese civilization to Japan, and in the course of several centuries Buddhism influenced not only Japanese religion and morality but also the politics of the country, for it helped to centralize the government, just as the government in China was formerly highly centralized.

By-and-by the chief ruler, known to the Japanese as the Kotei, and not the Mikado, as he is called by the foreigners, attained to absolute reign. This was accomplished with the aid of the military class. By the year 1200 A.D. it was the *shogun*, the chief of the most powerful tribe, who was the supreme ruler of Japan, the Kotei, or Mikado, being a mere figurehead. This feudal system prevailed through a number of centuries, with strong and influential barons, or *daimios* (written also *daimyos*), holding large estates and keeping armies of trained retainers, known as *samurai*, or soldiers, who developed the cult of honor, courage and loyalty.

Finally, in 1868, the Japanese nobles surrendered their hereditary rights to the Mikado, and at last, in 1889, Japan became a constitutional monarchy. This occurred when the emperor Matsuhito had begun to rule. His reign, known as *Meiji*, the *enlightened rule*, extended to 1912. His successor was Yoshihito, whose reign was known as *Taisho*, the *great righteousness*, and continued till 1926. Owing to the military class, which sought expansion, his rule became still more absolute, until Hirohito, whose reign was known as *Showo*, or *bright peace*, was fully worshiped as "god," an honor which also his predecessors had usurped.

To the great disappointment of the Japanese, the outcome of the Second World War proved that their emperor was not divine and that their army was not invincible.

These bits of Japanese history the reader must keep in mind in order to understand the history of Christian mission work in Japan.

THE ANCIENT RELIGIONS OF JAPAN

The oldest and, perhaps, indigenous, religion of Japan is *Shinto*, which has been interpreted to mean "the way of the gods." Shinto is a system of ancestral and nature worship, the elements of which, no doubt, were imported from China or Northern Asia by those who came from that country. Originally it seems to have had no explicit code of morals. Man was regarded as virtuous by nature, and his conscience was considered to be his supreme guide. Shinto professed existence beyond the grave, but had no theory as to rewards or punishments.

Shinto was absorbed by Buddhism, which came to Japan during the sixth century A.D. It was revived in 1868, when the people began to worship the emperor as a divine being, the direct descendant and actual representative of the sun-goddess, Amaterasu.

In the course of time Shinto developed a huge pantheon of more than eight million gods and goddesses and established temples, priests, forms of worship and rites, many of which were degrading, based on superstition and licentiousness. Its central tenet, however, especially as developed later, was implicit obedience to the Kotei, or Mikado. Since also in Japan pagan religion is syncretistic, being made up of various forms of idolatry, it is difficult to define pure Shinto beyond the general description given. For the average Japanese the highest form of worship was until recently absolute dedication to the emperor and the country.

Buddhism came to Japan from China by the way of Korea in 550 A.D., and is an aggressive, militant missionary religion. Several centuries passed before Buddhism became acceptable to the Japanese, and by that time it was so changed by adoption of Japanese religious principles and elements that it differed considerably from orthodox Continental Buddhism.

But Buddhism answered questions which the Japanese' own religious system had not definitely settled, as, for instance, those concerning the origin and destiny of human life. Today Buddhism, blended with elements of Shinto, wields a powerful influence over the people of Japan. It boasts of having thousands of temples, many of which are large and imposing, and copies from Christianity such things as are popular with the people, as, for example, Sunday schools, preaching on Sunday, young men's associations and the like. But Buddhism cannot conceal from discerning people its degrading evils, above all the vileness of its priests and worship and its inability to save the masses of Japan from utter degradation. It has become a vicious polytheistic, or even atheistic, religion, having no comfort for those that live and no hope for those that die, for, according to Buddhism, living means endless spiritual discipline by way of *karma*, or rebirth, until there comes at last the utter "blowing out," or the *Nirvana*, when existence ceases altogether.

As Buddhism, so also *Confucianism* has come to Japan from China. Confucianism itself is not fundamentally religious, but ethical. Whatever animistic or polydemonistic elements were engrafted upon it came to it by the way of syncretism. Master K'ung himself, or K'ung-fu-tse, who lived in China from 551 to 478 B.C., concerned himself only with moral precepts. The highest goal of his teaching was the welfare of the State, which, as he believed, could be obtained by keeping inviolate the five primary relationships of ruler and subject, father and son, husband and wife, elder and younger brother, friend and friend. Confucius also taught the virtues of sincerity, benevolence and filial love. However, he produced no theological system. In Japan, Confucianism has had a wholesome effect upon the people, inasmuch as it recalled to them the virtues of the divine law written in the human heart.

Although the Japanese language differs from that of China, Chinese is the language of Japanese literature and the Chinese classics have been read in the schools of Japan. This explains the far-reaching influence of the ethical system of Confucius in the Land of the Rising Sun.

From the little that has been said it is obvious to the reader that pagan religion cannot save Japan, for, negatively, it is nothing else than a fearful groping in spiritual darkness, and, positively, a worship of the powers of evil, connected with immorality and other shameful vices. Fortunately, Christianity has come, with its light of the Gospel of Jesus Christ, also to Japan.

CHRISTIANITY IN JAPAN

There is reason to assume that Christianity came to Japan already in the eighth century A.D., when Nestorian missionaries in China ventured beyond the sea that separated the Japanese island of Honshu from the mainland.

Be that as it may, the first modern missionary who brought Christianity to Japan was the Jesuit Francis Xavier, who landed in Japan in the year 1549. He remained in Japan for only two and a half years and never learned the Japanese language, so that he was sorely handicapped in his work.

Nevertheless, his success was phenomenal, especially since his friend and helper, Juan Fernandez, the real founder of Christianity in Japan, ably continued the work where Xavier left it. Other Jesuits followed, and later came Dominicans, Franciscans and Augustinians, so that by the year 1600 there were in Japan about 800,000 baptized Christians. But by that time persecutions began to set in, and in 1640 death was made the penalty by law of all those who embraced Christianity.

For nearly two centuries Japan now shut itself off from all Christian influences. But strange to say, when, after that long period of time, the country was again opened to Christian missions, there still were about 50,000 Christians, who, although ignorant of true Christianity, nevertheless retained teachings and practices handed down to them from that earlier Christian day; and this in spite of the fact that during the long and fierce persecution more than 300,000 Christians were put to death. The date, March 17, 1865, is now commemorated by "The Feast of the Finding of the Christians in Japan."

We owe the reopening of Japan to Christian missions to

Commodore Perry, who on July 8, 1853, dropped anchor in Yedo Bay and demanded an interview with the Japanese government. His efforts were not successful at once, but on March 31, 1854, an agreement was reached with the Japanese government by which the two ports of Shimoda and Hakodate were opened to American trade. Other treaties with other Christian nations followed, and before long, Protestant missionaries began to appear in Japan.

Even before this, in 1837, the ardent missionary Karl Guetzlaff had tried to evangelize Japan. Failing to accomplish anything, he made translations of some portions of the Bible, which he endeavored to spread in Japan. Later, from 1846 to 1853, Bettelheim, a converted Hungarian Jew, did mission work on Niukia, one of the Luchu Islands. But also these attempts met with failure.

The first Protestant missionary to arrive in Japan was the Rev. John Liggins of the Protestant Episcopal Church of America, who arrived in Japan on May 2, 1859. Almost lost in a pagan world, where as yet no religious freedom was known so far as Christianity was concerned, he nevertheless bravely attacked his difficult task, trying to win the people for Christianity by indirect methods, since he was not permitted to preach the Gospel.

About a month later he was joined by the Rev. C. M. Williams of the same denomination, who labored so tactfully and discreetly that his influence became far-reaching and he later was appointed bishop of Yedo, as the city of Tokyo then was called. Both missionaries were Americans.

In October, 1859, Dr. J. C. Hepburn, a medical missionary, and his wife came to Japan and developed a long and useful missionary activity. He was sent by the American Presbyterian Board, which later sent out many other able and successful missionaries.

In November, 1859, there landed in Japan two missionaries of the Reformed Church of America, the Rev. S. R. Brown and the Rev. D. B. Simmons, two pioneer workers who did much to pave the way for later missionaries. A week later, in November, 1859, there arrived at Japan the great and influential missionary, the Rev. Guido F. Verbeck, who was also of the Reformed Church of America, and who, perhaps, was the most successful of these early missionaries.

The American Baptist Free Missionary Society, early in 1860, sent to Japan their first worker, the consecrated Rev. J. Goble, who had been with Perry's expedition and was, therefore, well acquainted with Japanese ways and conditions. It is remarkable that within four months from the opening of Japan to foreign residents there arrived in the country seven American missionaries, and equally remarkable it is that within a year after the treaty, four American mission societies had begun work there.

Of course, the work of these and other early missionaries was not easy. The years 1859 to 1873 constitute a "period of preparation," during which Japan was prepared for Christianity. As yet the missionaries were not allowed to proclaim the Gospel and win converts openly. Their activity was limited to literary work, and especially the teaching of English and of Western sciences. The Japanese were always curious to hear something new, being very desirous of learning just what made the Western nations so powerful as indeed they were. The missionaries exercised personal influence also through the practice of medicine as well as through their personal conduct, by which they greatly impressed the Japanese.

It is characteristic of the Japanese that they called their Country *Dai Nippon*, which means, roughly translated, the "great land of the rising sun." From this name of their country, the Japanese are also known as the Nipponese, though the term *Japanese* is generally used.

The period from 1873 to 1879 is known as the "period of progress." By this time the people of Japan, and especially the government of Japan, had become so favorably impressed with Christianity as a dynamic factor for good that formal opposition to Christian mission work gradually ceased, the stringent edicts against the new Western religion being removed. However, while preaching of the Divine Word was permitted, the freedom of religion, which was guaranteed to the Christians, was only relative, and powerful groups still identified Christianity with everything that was anti-Japanese. The reason for this is clear, for as Christianity was spread in Japan, the ancient pagan religions of Shintoism, Buddhism and Confucianism were revived, and since emperor worship was now inculcated in the people by the military class, Shintoism, with which Christianity could not agree, became its most dangerous and effectual rival. Still, Christianity, by its very divine power, continued to gain friends in Japan, especially as its advocates were linked with the element of civic, scientific, social and economic progress.

The time from 1889 to 1941 may be called the "period of reaction," since during these years Japan, coming into its own as a powerful nation, resented all foreign influences and became stupidly nationalistic and chauvinistic. There appeared a lamentable jealousy of all foreigners, just as in China. Then, too, the friction among the various denominations with their differing doctrines increased the hatred which the Japanese felt toward foreigners in general. There was much criticism of missionary methods by Japanese who had been educated abroad, especially since modern religious liberalism, which did so much injury to the churches at home, gradually perverted the missionary forces which, instead of confessing Christ and His Gospel in its whole truth and purity, became syncretistic and often fellowshiped with those very pagan opponents whose wrong and injurious tenets the early missionaries had tried to expose to the people. As Christianity became liberal in its teaching and practice, it became weak and met with the contempt of such Christian Japanese leaders as were not in agreement with its policy of religious appeasement.

In spite of all this, however, we must not regard the preaching of the Gospel in Japan as having been without fruit. The Scriptural doctrine of the election to eternal life is most comforting and encouraging to Christian missionaries. Paul speaks of this doctrine thus: "The election hath obtained . . . and the rest were blinded" (Rom. 11:7), the latter not because of any lack of divine mercy, but because they rejected the counsel of God against themselves (Acts 7:51; Luke 7:30). No matter where Christian missionaries toil in the Lord's vineyard, the elect will always obtain salvation, and the elect are those who in simple childlike faith accept the precious Gospel of Christ (Isa. 55:11); and no matter how strongly men may oppose the message of life, wherever the Gospel is being preached, God's house is being filled with happy, grateful worshipers. What Christianity today must give to Japan is more than mere externals, such as education, medical service, political direction and the like. Japan needs the precious Gospel of the world's Redeemer and through Him the hope of eternal salvation with visions of comfort in life's manifold and many ills. We are rightly oriented to this world only if we are rightly oriented to our Father's house in heaven; and we are rightly oriented to man only if we are rightly oriented to God.

In the course of time virtually all Christian denominations of our own country and others have performed mission service in Japan. While it is difficult in so brief an overview as this, to state details, the educational work of the Methodists might be singled out as outstanding, though also the other church bodies established lower and higher schools in Japan. In fact, mission work has been carried on in Japan largely by education, since that proved itself the easiest and most practical approach. But education has not solved the problem of bringing Christ to Japan, for a recent religious census at the University of Tokyo showed the following: agnostics, 3,000; atheists, 1,500; Buddhists, 300; Christians, 30; Shintoists, 8; Confucianists, 6. While statistics are never reliable, they nevertheless give a fair picture, in general, of prevailing conditions.

Lutherans from Finland established mission work in Japan in 1902. Lutherans from America came to Japan in 1892, 1898, 1908 and in the following years their work was both educational and evangelistic, but was never done on a larger scale. What Japan needs above all is old-fashioned evangelism in the true sense of the term— the simple witness of Jesus Christ as the Hope of the world.

The first recorded Protestant convert in Japan was Yano Rinzan, who was baptized in November, 1864. The next were two brothers, Murata Wasaka and Ayoba, both noble men of the government. They were baptized by the great missionary Verbeck in May, 1866.

If the reader will find the names of many great missionaries, of whom he has heard or whom he even knows personally, omitted, let him take into consideration the lack of space which forbids the recitation of many names and works which rightfully should be honored. In the mission history of Japan there loom such great names as those of D. C. Greene, J. D. Davis, J. T. Gulick, J. C. Berry, W. S. Clark, L. L. Janes and John Batchelor, who laid the firm foundation for the work among the Ainu, primitive folk in Hokkaido, though mission work was begun there already in the 1870's, and scores of others. If men must pass over their names and work, the eternal, just Lord of the harvest will not forget their endeavors on behalf of His kingdom, and in the eternal home of Christ's saints and heroes they will find their rich reward of grace. Then, perhaps, it will appear, too, that the unknown workers have often been the best, the most faithful, the most deserving, though their work was not acknowledged on earth.

It would lead us too far afield were we to describe

the effort of uniting the various Protestant denominations in Japan into one large native church. But this endeavor seemed all the more necessary since the Japanese keenly felt their national consciousness from the beginning. In 1877 the *Nippon Kirisuto Itchi Kyokwai,* the United Church of Christ in Japan, was constituted by denominations which professed the Reformed faith. This later became the *Nippon Kirisuto Kyokwai,* the Church of Christ in Japan. Other similar church unions followed, until the Second World War brought about the *Kyodan,* the union of virtually all Protestant churches in Japan. This worked a hardship for strictly confessing churches, and, no doubt, many will withdraw when opportunity will be granted them, as several societies have already done at this writing. While true unity in Christendom is highly desirable and urgently demanded in Scripture, a mere external union, which permits liberalism and neglect of Christian doctrine to prevail and forces conscientious Christians to stifle their confessions, making hypocrites out of them, cannot be a blessing to men. There is only one thing that makes Christians strong, and that is unity of spirit, wrought by the Holy Ghost through the common faith in Christ. This spiritual, inward unity is much more effective than any mere external union can be.

Unfortunately, church statistics in Japan have never been complete and accurate, and during the last decades circumstances have well-nigh prevented the completion of dependable statistics. In 1919 church reports showed the following in Japan: 1,150 Protestant churches; 117,000 native Christians, including all baptized persons; 1,100 foreign missionaries; 4,200 native pastors and workers. When one estimates the population of Japan at 98,000,000, or even at 75,000,000, these figures teach a pitiful, tragic lesson. Must Christianity in Japan forever remain the religion of a small minority? Will not the ardent prayers and self-sacrificial endeavors of earnest Christians in America and Europe bring about a greater harvest in this land whose population shows much interest in the material things which Western civilization has to offer to them? Certainly Japan is worth evangelizing! And it is for our own well-being and prosperity that we bring to Japan at this time, when the Gospel will find ready ears, the saving truth that is in Christ Jesus.

We know, of course, that much more has been accomplished in Japan than figures can show. The Lord's kingdom does not come with pomp and show. In His quiet, hidden manner, the Lord Jesus still walks about in the Judaeas, the Samarias and the Galilees of our modern world, claiming through His Word, preached by humble missionaries and exemplified in their lives, the elect, whom the Father has given to Him from eternity. His kingdom is not of this world, but it is in this world, and it is a world-kingdom, though our mortal eyes cannot as yet behold its transcendent glory.

And so we ardently pray, "Thy kingdom come!"

2

The Beautiful Island of Taiwan

(Formosa)

THE COUNTRY AND ITS PEOPLE

EVEN THOUGH the island of Formosa is small and relatively unimportant so far as missionary success is concerned, it deserves a separate place in this general introductory overview because it challenges our interest as a land in which much mission work can still be accomplished, indeed, to state the situation frankly, in which mission work has hardly begun.

The island of Formosa, called by the Japanese and the Chinese *Taiwan,* received its name from the Portuguese who settled there in 1590. They were so enchanted by the island that they called it the "Beautiful," for this is the meaning of *Formosa.*

It is about 250 miles long and from 50 to 70 miles wide, and is separated from China by the Formosa Strait. Its area is about 14,000 square miles and its population is a little more than 5,000,000. Its interior is mountainous, and its plains slope gently from the mountains to the sea.

Formosa is indeed a pleasant island in many respects, highly esteemed both by the Chinese and Japanese, though its climate is warm and also malarial. It has much rugged mountain scenery and many beautiful valleys. Its tillable soil produces rich and varied crops. No wonder that many nations have fought for it.

After the Portuguese had held Formosa for a time, they had to yield it to the Spaniards, who in turn had to cede it to the Dutch, those intrepid seafarers who occupied it in 1624. In 1683 the island became a part of the Chinese empire, but in 1895, at the close of the war between China and Japan, China had to surrender it to the Japanese.

Of the 5,000,000 people living in Formosa, the majority are Chinese. But since 1895 many Japanese have settled in the coast towns where they have engaged chiefly in trade. The aborigines are Malay in origin, and in the mountains in which they reside they retain their savage customs, even that of human head-hunting. They often descend from their mountain retreats, attack the valley population and usually return with rich supplies of spoil. All attempts to subdue or even to exterminate them have failed. They are in Taiwan not to be destroyed but to be evangelized, and that is the task of the Christian Church today.

THE RELIGION OF PAGAN TAIWAN

Little need be said about the pagan religion of those who inhabit Formosa. The Chinese are Buddhist and Confucianists, and the Japanese are Shintoists also in Taiwan, just as in their home country. The aborigines, who are said to be related to the Malays of Borneo and like them are extremely cruel, have primitive religious concepts. Their worship is, in the main, spirit worship, and they are said to entertain a dreadful fear of the evil spirits, which they believe inhabit the mountains, causing human beings as much unhappiness as possible and daily seeking to take their lives. The evil spirits must, therefore, be appeased and the good spirit invoked for protection. Savagery, superstition, immorality and utter hopelessness characterize also these unfortunate heathen, into whose life the light of Christ has not shone, and who, bearing the common ills of humanity, have no comfort to console them against the spiritual ills of the soul, the anguish of life and the agony of death.

Certainly in our intercessions we should remember also these unfortunates who should share in the blessings of redemption, just as we, who have been enriched with the Divine Word, partake of the grace of our Saviour.

CHRISTIANITY IN TAIWAN

When in 1624 the Dutch took over Formosa, here also they followed their policy of doing mission work among those over whom they ruled. During the many years when they occupied the island they sent about thirty missionaries there, who translated portions of the Bible into the vernacular used by the natives and baptized about 6,000 converts. The power of the Divine Word is proved by the fact that when in 1715 the famous Jesuit scientist and missionary de Mailla came to Formosa he found traces of that early mission work; for, as he relates, many natives abhorred the idols, professed belief in the triune God, knew the story of the fall of our first parents, knew the baptismal formula and the meaning of baptism, and readily took to Christian instruction. This report may, of course, be somewhat exaggerated, but there can be no doubt that it is true in its essential features. Christianity has a strange way of surviving under adverse circumstances. It did so in Japan, and no doubt also in Formosa.

Protestant mission work was begun in Formosa in 1865, when missionaries from the English Presbyterian Church came to the island. They chose for their field the central and southwestern part of the island. The Canadian Presbyterian Church has labored on the island since 1872. Their pioneer missionary was Rev. G. L. Mackay, who worked there from 1872 to 1901. The Canadian Presbyterians chose for their field the northern part of Formosa. Both of these mission societies worked among the Chinese and the aborigines, though to this day no work has been undertaken among the natives living in the interior. Since Japan has taken over Formosa, Christian mission work has been done also among them, Japanese Christians laboring among the Japanese colonists, though with little success.

A great difficulty arose for the mission schools in Formosa when the Japanese government, after having taken the island, introduced its own school system, in which the pupils were required to observe political Shinto. The same, of course, was demanded also of the mission schools, and while the government declared that this was only a patriotic expression, it, in reality, involved an idolatrous recognition of the Japanese emperor as a god. The Canadian Presbyterian Mission, therefore, closed its schools rather than conform to this law.

In 1912 a union was affected between the Canadian and the English Presbyterian missions, which together at that time represented a Christian church of more than 30,000 members. In 1938 there were, roughly speaking, about 50,000 Christians on the island. At the same time it was reported that the non-Christian people were increasing much faster than the Christian. What a challenge this means for us to whom the Lord's work is precious!

The difficulty of the Christian work is Formosa may be learned from the following. The aborigines consist of nine tribes, each of which speaks its own dialect. These natives number about 150,000, but they live in more than 700 villages, most of which have no connection at all with each other. Some of these are difficult to reach, and others are almost inaccessible. Such is the task that awaits us on the beautiful island of Taiwan.

3

The Land of the Morning Calm

(Korea)

THE COUNTRY AND ITS PEOPLE

THE ANCIENT NAME of Korea is *Chosen,* and this means
"morning calm." The name is still used by the natives,
though it was conferred on their country by the Chinese
about twelve hundred years before Christ.

The term "Korea" comes from *Korai,* which is the
designation of the northernmost of three states that were
united into the one country of Korea many centuries ago.
Since Korea has been shut off from other nations and
existed for centuries in utter seclusion, it has also been
called the "Hermit Nation."

Korea is a peninsula about 650 miles long, reaching
out into the Pacific Ocean from the mainland of Manchuria. It is separated from China by the Yellow Sea
and from Japan by the Sea of Japan. Along its southern
shore there lie many islands, some of which, however, are
rather small. Korea is about 135 miles wide and has
a coast line of 1,750 miles. Altogether its area is about
86,000 square miles. That means that about three Koreas
could be placed in the state of Texas.

The situation and the seclusion of Korea have had a

30

remarkable influence upon its people, which number about 23,000,000. Korea's ports were closed to Europeans and Americans alike, until in 1882, Commodore Shufeldt of the United States Navy succeeded in securing a treaty. This was the first treaty of friendship and commerce ever signed by Korea with a Western power, and its modern history begins with this late date.

In the main, Korea is mountainous. Its long coast line presents an uninviting approach from the sea. However, in the interior there are many fertile hills and pleasant valleys in which rice, as well as other grains, vegetables and fruits are grown. There is much charming hill and mountain scenery and Seoul, the capital, has been described as one of the most beautifully situated cities in the world. The number of Korea's large cities is very small. Most of the people live in tiny houses and lead a primitive and laborious life; they are ever patient and hard-working and easily satisfied with simple returns from their labors. Farming methods are still primitive, but usually enough food is raised to feed the millions of this strange land. Frequently there is even enough left for export.

The climate of Korea is, on the whole, salubrious. The summers are temperate and the winters are cold, though never unbearably so. The mean summer temperature is seventy-five, the mean winter temperature, thirty-three. But for about two months during the summer there is a rainy season which brings the precipitation up to 30 or 40 inches. The rain then falls almost incessantly and the climate is hot and sultry. Fortunately there are many mountain resorts where people may then find refuge.

Korea has about 11,000 miles of poor cart roads and about 3,000 miles of railroads. Among its exports are such natural resources as timber, coal, iron, crystal, talc, copper and gold. Other exports are rice, grains, fruits, cotton, paper, ginseng, beans, peas and the like. There is a great opportunity for enterprising Western nations to develop the mining of the rich mineral resources of this great country, which so far have been greatly neglected.

The origin of the Koreans and their language has been lost in history, but no doubt they are of Mongoloid derivation. In general, the Koreans resemble the Mongolians. They are larger than the Japanese but smaller than the northern Chinese. They generally have good physique, strength and endurance. While the cast of mind in China is commercial and that in Japan is military, in Korea it is literary, so that Korea represents a nation of scholars. The first impression which Europeans gained of the Koreans was rather negative, for they described the people as lazy, dishonest, slovenly in person and habits, and worthy of but little respect. But this verdict has been declared to be too severe and even unfair, and those who now write of the Koreans usually speak of them in very favorable terms, especially of those who have become Westernized and Christianized.

The language of Korea resembles both the Chinese and the Japanese, and yet also differs from them. It has an alphabet which is made up of twenty-five letters, but in addition to the native script, the people, just as in Japan, also use the Chinese ideographs, and the Chinese classics have furnished the basis of the literary education of the people for centuries.

Bits of Korean History

One reason why Korea secluded itself from other countries was its fear of warfare. The Koreans are not a military but a peace-loving people. Still, this simple, peaceably-inclined country for centuries became a prey to her stronger rival neighbors simply because of her location.

To the Chinese, Korea was known a thousand years before Christ. In about 1100 B.C. a Chinese nobleman, fearing the wrath of the emperor, is said to have fled to Korea with 5,000 retainers and made his home there.

Later, intertribal wars occurred, during which the warring parties called upon China and Japan for help so that the country suffered from endless strife and subjugation. In 1281 Kublai Khan compelled the Koreans to assist him in his war on Japan, which failed. In return, the Koreans were attacked by the Japanese so that much bitterness has prevailed between the two nations.

In 1592 Japan made an unsuccessful attempt to conquer Korea. The efficient but cruel Japanese general Hideyoshi overran the country to make it a highway toward the conquest of China. His ruthless warfare took a dreadful toll of life. He sent to Japan enormous quantities of booty and maltreated the people horribly by cutting off their ears and noses and sending them to Japan as tokens of his military success. But supported by the Chinese, the Koreans finally defeated their enemies and drove them back with terrible loss. No wonder Korea closed its ports to foreign nations after that.

Early in the seventeenth century there occurred the struggle between China and the Manchus, which ended in the seating of a Manchu ruler upon the Chinese throne. Korea was invaded and placed under tribute.

In 1894 war broke out between Japan and China with Korea as the battleground and bone of contention. China was defeated and Korea made subject to Japan. Next appeared the Russians, who were defeated by Japan in the war of 1904-1905. This led to the formal annexation of Korea to Japan in 1910. Ever since, until the end of the Second World War, in 1945, Japan was dominant in Korea and forced upon it the Japanese language, laws, school system, religion and whatever the military class of Japan, which then ruled the country, decreed. Today helpless, peaceful Korea is threatened by Russian totalitarianism, and what the future may have to offer to this unfortunate country remains to be seen. May Christianity so steel the hearts of the people that they will find strength to bear all afflictions and in their tribulation show themselves more than conquerors.

THE ANCIENT RELIGIONS OF KOREA

As in China and Japan, so also in Korea, pagan religion is syncretistic, that is, a mixture of many beliefs. The oldest religion in Korea is, perhaps, Shamanism, which is the common cult of the uncivilized tribes of Northern Asia. The word is derived from the term *shaman*, meaning "priest," or "medicine man," who acts as the medium, exorcist or conjurer to influence the good and evil spirits which bless or trouble the people. In China, Shamanism is known as *Chiao*, which means "yellow sect," a term derived from the yellow color of the priestly robes, a *shaman* being a holy man, or a person who has overcome all fleshly passions. The term is said to be Hindu in its origin, for the idea of a holy man, appearing in yellow robes, is native to India. Shamanism in Korea has become a mass of grotesque superstitions by means of which the good spirits are invoked, while the evil spirits are propitiated by offerings and works.

Buddhism came to Korea in the fourth century of our Lord's era and was later introduced into Japan from this country. It gained great power, but because the Buddhist priests meddled in politics, it was placed under the ban and was not restored until 1895 when the pro-Japanese party came into power. But Buddhism thrived throughout the centuries by its many and well-endowed monasteries and was held in high honor by the common people, and especially, too, by the women of Korea.

Confucianism, which came to Korea from China, has done much to mold the moral thought and life of the nation. It came to Korea at a very early time and its literature was deeply appreciated by its people. However, since it is fundamentally an ethical code and properly not a religion, it did nothing to elevate the religious thought of the Koreans. While the chief rite of ancestral worship is observed throughout the land, Confucianism properly became the moral code of the more educated of Korea's people.

In a general way, however, syncretism characterizes the religious belief of the pagan Koreans. Shamanistic, Buddhistic, Shintoistic and Confucianistic trends prevail in the common beliefs of the people, especially of those who do considerable reading, and, in general, the Koreans love to read and study. This explains also the ready acceptation of Christianity in the Land of the Morning Calm.

CHRISTIANITY IN KOREA

Strange to say, it was the conquering Japanese army that was the first to bring Christianity to Korea; for when in 1592, Hideyoshi went to the peninsula to conquer it, there were many Christians in his army, the fruits of the successful Jesuit mission of that century. In 1593, at the request of some of the Christian Japanese officers, a European Jesuit and a Japanese lay brother were assigned to minister to the soldiers, and they reached Korea in 1594. Several converts were baptized, but the charge was raised against the Jesuit priest that he was fomenting sedition and so he was called back to Japan.

Soon afterward a number of Korean slaves in Nagasaki, the center of Christianity in Japan at that time, were converted and baptized. During the severe persecutions which befell the Christians in Japan, these Korean Christians proved themselves faithful, and they preferred to die rather than give up their faith.

It was through the Jesuits in China that the Koreans later made further contact with Christianity, for when ambassadors were sent from Korea to Peking, these read some of Ricci's treatises on Christianity, and about the year 1770 at least one of these ambassadors was converted to Christianity, though he was never baptized.

So much is certain that in 1784 Christianity became a continuing power in Korea. In that year Thomas Kim, the son of a Korean ambassador to Peking, who had been baptized in China, returned to his home country to begin mission work there. In 1795 a Chinese Catholic priest, Father Tsiou, followed and, in disguise, worked among the people. There were at that time about 4,000 converts in the country, as Catholic records show. In 1829 a Catholic foreign mission society in Paris took over the difficult work. No sooner had Christianity become known in Korea than persecutions ensued, and it is estimated that to 1870 at least 8,000 Christian converts died as martyrs. But though the persecutions were long and severe, the Christian religion remained in Korea, and today there are more than 200,000 Catholics in that country.

Protestant mission work began successfully in Korea soon after the treaty had been established with the United States through Commodore Shufeldt in 1882. Before this, however, the ardent missionary Guetzlaff had circulated religious tracts among Koreans in their language. In 1866 R. J. Thomas, a Scottish Presbyterian missionary, had lost his life in attempting to start mission work in Korea. A similar fate befell a traveling secretary of the Bible Society, Alexander Williamson. In 1873 John Ross labored among Koreans living in Manchuria, for whom he translated portions of the Bible, which later a Korean convert, Yikuitai, spread in his home country, thus preparing the way for American mission work.

As in Japan so also in Korea mission history may be divided into three periods. The first marks the *beginning* of Christian work and extends to the end of the Sino-Japanese war in 1896. The second period, extending to 1910, was one of marvelous *advance*, during which thousands of Koreans were converted. The third dates from

Japan's annexation of Korea in 1910 and is marked by great difficulties placed in the way of Christianity's onward march.

In 1884 the Northern Presbyterian Board appointed the Rev. J. W. Heron, M. D., a medical missionary, to Korea, but when his departure was delayed, Dr. H. N. Allen of the same board, who was already in China, was transferred to Korea and thus became the first Protestant missionary to reach the Land of the Morning Calm. His medical skill and successful operations soon made him popular in court circles, but unfortunately for Christian mission work he was later prevailed upon to enter the diplomatic service.

In 1885 there arrived in Korea the Rev. H. G. Underwood, sent by the Northern Presbyterian Board. He remained in Korea for thirty-one years, during which he founded and presided over the Chosen Christian College, prepared a Korean-English dictionary, assisted in translating the Bible and pioneered in the preparation of Christian literature of all kinds.

In the same year, 1885, there arrived in Korea also the Rev. H. G. Appenzeller and Dr. W. B. Scranton, who were sent by the Methodist Episcopal Board. Their sending was induced largely by the successful work and the glowing mission reports of the Rev. R. S. Maclay, who in the 1880's was superintendent of the Methodist missions in Japan. As early as 1872, he had interested himself in mission work in Korea, and in 1884 he was granted permission to enter that country for considering the prospects for mission work there. He thus divides with Dr. Allen the honor of being the first Christian American missionary to visit Korea; but since he did not remain in Korea, the honor of being the first permanent missionary in Korea belongs to Dr. Allen.

On July 11, 1886, the first Protestant Korean convert, No Tohsa, was baptized, the first of thousands who were soon to follow. Because of the danger connected with the public confession of Christ at that time, he was baptized in secret, though afterward the young Korean church bravely confessed its faith before its enemies.

There is a most interesting record of a communion service, which took place privately in Mr. Underwood's home and was the first ever held in Korea. It was held in December, 1887, and was attended by seven communicants.

Meanwhile other mission societies sent their representatives to Korea. The Young Men's Christian Association of the University of Toronto in 1888 sent out the brilliant writer the Rev. James S. Gale, who later joined the Presbyterian mission. Afterward he distinguished himself by writing numerous books on Korea and its missionary opportunities, describing winsomely the land and its people. His works are still being read by friends of the Korean missions, and while times have changed greatly since he came to Korea, the mission background has remained largely the same to this day.

In 1889 the Australian Presbyterians took up work in Korea. They were followed in 1890 by the English Episcopalians. The Southern Presbyterians came in 1892, the Southern Methodists in 1896 and the Canadian Presbyterians in 1898, so that at that early date the entire land was filled with the Gospel.

At first the work was very hard. The law which has been passed against the Roman Catholic Christians remained in force for a long time, and consequently the Protestant converts were never safe. In addition to this, in 1884 a reform party attempted to overthrow the reactionary Korean government, and this created confusion and uncertainty everywhere. The internal divisions in the country injured Christian mission work directly, for the foes of the missions were thus given an opportunity to oppose the activity of the missionaries.

To 1890 the work in Korea had been confined to one

station, which was situated in Seoul. By 1891 the number
of Korean Christians, ready to profess the faith, numbered
no more than about one hundred, but gradually the missions branched out. A successful station was opened soon
afterward in Pyeng Yang. In the course of time the progress of Protestant Christianity in Korea became so rapid
and extensive that Korea has been called the "Miracle of
Modern Missions." As mission society after society appealed to the country, a nation-wide interest in Christianity was created among rich and poor, learned and
unlearned, and there was a Pentecostal outpouring of the
Spirit such as few other countries experienced.

There are a number of causes for this joyous and
enthusiastic reception of the Christian faith.

In the first place, many Koreans, no doubt, were tired of
the hollow, helpless ancient religions which had prevailed
in their country and had helped neither to make the land
safe nor to render the people courageous. Against the
fighting Japanese and the aggressive Chinese the Koreans
found themselves helpless to defend their country. Christianity offered to the distressed and perplexed people a new
vision of honor and glory, together with new ideals for
which to work and fight.

Then also it cannot be denied that the Koreans, ever
eager to learn, were greatly attracted by the Christian
Bible and other edifying mission literature which the
missionaries brought to them. In the past the Koreans
had been nurtured on Chinese religious books, which,
after all, could give them neither comfort nor guidance,
and above all, could not answer the baffling questions that
faced them as individuals and as a nation. It is quite
natural, therefore, that this "nation of scholars" should
readily turn to a book so unique in every way, and, besides,
so full of strength and inspiration, as the Holy Bible.

No doubt, too, the personality and the conduct of the
early pioneer missionaries had much to do with making

Christianity acceptable to the Koreans. The medical missionaries, in this land of much and grievous illness, startled the Koreans into attention by their remarkable cures of much sickness which had defied their medicinemen for centuries. But the nonmedical missionaries were also so altogether dedicated to the cause of their Saviour that as the heathen perceived the radiance of their consecration they were led to follow and imitate them. They preached the Word not only by word, but also by their great sincerity, self-denial and devotion to their sacred task.

Lastly, there was the famous Nevius plan, or method, simple and natural indeed, but sorely neglected in many other mission fields.

Dr. J. L. Nevius, of Chefoo, China, came to Korea in 1890, where he explained to the missionaries his special method of doing mission work. The purpose of this method was to create a self-supporting and self-propagating native church.

According to this plan, each converted Christian was to remain in the calling in which he was called, but to use that calling as a means of spreading the Divine Word. The humble convert would thus work among his lowly fellow servants. The educated convert was to use his learning to win the literate for Christ. The rich was to win the rich, and the poor, the poor.

Whatever expense the mission entailed was to be borne by the native Christians, who were to "live within their income," setting up only such machinery as it could manage. Each church was to provide its own buildings for church and school purposes, the buildings to remain plain and simple and within the limit of the congregation's resources, so that all debts would be avoided.

Christian converts who showed special aptitude for evangelistic work were to be selected and supported by the native congregations, each regarding the work of the evangelists as its own, so that there would prevail among all Christians the feeling of pride, personal responsibility and immediate interest in the work. The whole plan was based upon sound psychology and it proved itself a great success in Korea, when once it was thoroughly understood.

Perhaps even more than the Nevius plan, the missionaries' emphasis on Bible study in large classes of old and young contributed toward the success of the Korean mission. From the very start the Koreans evinced a lively interest in the study of Scripture, and when they were organized into Bible-study classes, the response was most gratifying. In 1907, for example, 191 such classes were held in the Pyeng Yang station, and these were attended by more than 10,000 persons. In 1927 there were 541 classes, attended by 11,325 women and 7,754 men. There is no doubt that the study of the Bible did much to make Christianity popular in the Land of the Morning Calm. The Korean converts were true Bible Christians.

While the mission work in Korea was largely evangelistic, Christian education was not lost sight of. Each congregation was encouraged to maintain a Christian day school and to support its teaching staff. In 1907 there were more than 300 such primary Christian day schools, all of which were virtually self-supporting.

The graduates of the primary schools were instructed in secondary schools where they were trained in Biblical and secular lore. These secondary schools helped to displace the ancient study of Chinese literature and pointed the students to new and greater objectives in life. Since the instruction was based upon a substantial Christian foundation, it proved itself a powerful factor in dispelling the pessimistic, defeatistic philosophy which the Koreans had imbibed through the study of the Chinese classics. Christianity gave them a new outlook on life.

By 1907 there were more than 1,000 self-supporting churches in Korea, with about 30,000 communicants and more than 120,000 adherents. In that year these churches contributed toward church and mission needs about $80,000 in United States money, a large sum indeed when one considers the poverty of the average Korean and the low value of their currency.

By 1910 the number of Christian adherents had increased to 178,686. There were then 34 ordained Korean ministers and 1,897 catechists. The Sunday-school enrollment soared to 400,000 attendants. Some of the large city churches had as many as 3,000 Sunday-school students.

Church prayer meetings became extremely popular among the Koreans, some churches recording average regular attendances of 1,500 and more. The church at Pyeng Yang was, perhaps, the most richly blessed in this fruit of faith.

However, the Korean churches did not only support home missions but also engaged in foreign mission efforts. They launched missions in such foreign countries as Manchuria, Hawaii, Mexico and the Pacific coast of the United States. They have begun mission work in the Shantung province, China, where they labor in more than twenty centers and have baptized more than 1,000 converts. Thus by preaching Christ in the land of their benefactors the Koreans repaid the people who were the first to bring them Christianity. A noble gesture indeed, and what is more, an expression of genuine Christian gratitude!

We shall not speak of the tribulation which befell the Church in Korea when in 1910 the Japanese annexed that country. The thirty-five years of Japanese dominion over the Land of the Morning Calm proved a period of severe testing and continual trial to the Korean Christians. In 1919, for example, the Federal Council of Churches of Christ in America published reports showing that at that time 631 Koreans were killed, 28,934 were arrested, 10,592 were flogged and released, and 5,156 were sent to prison. Japan, of course, speaks of these Koreans as political offenders, but while this is true in general, for they were, no doubt, engaged in the "passive resistance uprising" or "national declaration of independence," Japanese terrorism also had a religious aspect, for it attempted to force the Koreans to renounce their Christian faith and to honor the political and religious Shinto which the Japanese enforced upon the conquered land.

How the Japanese oppression affected the Christian missions is obvious from the following facts. Christian missionaries, foreign and native, were insulted and injured; seventeen churches were totally destroyed, while twenty-four others were badly damaged. In 1919 the Presbyterians reported that in their field alone 336 ministers, elders and helpers had been arrested. In addition, 2,125 male and 531 female church members were put into prison, 41 were shot and killed, 6 were beaten to death and 1,642 were made to languish in prison without a fair trial. Other mission societies and churches suffered in a similar way. No doubt there were many other casualties, but the Japanese militarists exercised a most severe military censorship, so that the outside world was kept ignorant of many of the crimes which were perpetrated upon the unfortunate Korean Christians.

In 1919, moved largely by the general world-protests, the Japanese government recalled its cruel military governor general from Korea and placed the country in charge of Baron Saito, a more peaceable and just man. The military police was then abolished, together with the system of torture employed by it, while the Koreans were granted more freedom and Christian missions received greater consideration. This more equitable treatment was the fruit also of the Korean independence movement, which became all the stronger as the policy of the conquerors became unbearable.

What is the mission outlook in Korea today? A new foe is now threatening oppressed Korea, and this foe is as tyrannical and antimission as was military Japan, perhaps even more so. But the Korean Church has proved itself constant and faithful, and it deserves the most loyal support of all Christian denominations. The Korean Christian Church has been tried by fire and has not been found wanting. It is ours today to see to it that the 500,000 and more Korean church members are not only kept in the faith but are also energized to carry on the work in the great tribulation awaiting them in the future. Let us unite our prayers also for Korea, where God has wrought wondrous deeds of salvation.

Statistics of Korean mission results are very inaccurate and incomplete, but in 1939 the *Statistical Survey of the World Mission* published the following report: 17 societies at work; 462 foreign missionaries; 63 resident stations; 6,283 paid native workers; 4,421 organized churches and other groups; 148,677 communicant members. The total number of Protestant adherents has been estimated as between 400,000 and 500,000.

It may be added that about the year 1900 a mission of the Russian Orthodox Church was begun at Seoul. Missions were founded also among Korean immigrants in Russian territory near the Korean border. By 1904 these mission endeavors had won about eight or nine thousand converts. These Russian mission endeavors, of course, were greatly harmed by the victory of Japan in 1905, but even in 1914 the Orthodox Church reported about 4,000 converts in nine stations.

4

Rimitsu, the Nestorian Physician

(724 - 748)

(WENT TO JAPAN IN 724)

THERE IS A REPORT, or, rather, a tradition, that a Nestorian physician, bearing the Japanese name Rimitsu, came to Japan when the emperor Shomu was ruling there. This would give him a service period of at least twenty-four years, or from 724 to 748.

Little is known about this early Christian missionary in Japan, and much of what is said concerning his work is legendary. But what is reported of him agrees with the mission interest and activity of the Nestorians in general, and, in particular, with their ability to influence by means of their learning leading persons through whom they worked to make known the Christian message of salvation in foreign lands. The Nestorians certainly were aggressive, enterprising missionaries, who came not only to India but also to China, and, no doubt, also to Japan.

We sometimes think of these Far Eastern countries as hopelessly shut off from the Christian message during the early years of the Christian Church. It is true, so far as reliable records are concerned, there is little to prove in detail that Christianity there became permanently established.

But if tradition means anything, we may assume that Christianity was brought to India, and even to China, by either Thomas the Apostle or by those who were influenced or converted by him. Intercourse between the nations in those early times was not so limited as we today are inclined to think. Alexander of Greece certainly could not have penetrated so far east had there not been trade routes and military roads which he was able to use. If Paul, writing to the Romans about 60 A.D. or earlier, could say, "Their sound [the glad Gospel tidings] went into all the earth, and their words unto the ends of the world" (Rom. 10:18), and again, writing to the Colossians about 64 A.D. or even earlier, "Which [the Gospel] is come unto you, as it is in all the world" (Col. 1:6), then certainly it is not incredible that the Gospel might have reached India, China and Japan by the year 300 A.D., or even earlier, so that in the fifth or sixth century when the Nestorians began their trek east, they were guided by definite Christian legends and traditions. The Nestorian tablet, found in 1625, near the present city of Sian in west China, clearly proves that the "illustrious doctrine" of Christianity had been spread far and wide in China by 781 A.D., and that it might have been carried before that time by Rimitsu into Japan. Christianity must have been firmly planted in the Far East, otherwise Marco Polo, visiting that faraway country in the thirteenth century, could not have alluded to the Nestorian churches as being numerous. Had they been few in number and weak in organization they would not have survived the terrific pounding of the continued persecution which befell them when emperors who hated Christianity occupied the throne.

Be that as it may, the report that Rimitsu reached Japan by 724 is certainly interesting. It is remarkable, too, that the wife of Emperor Shomu, brilliant Empress Komyo, bore the title "Light and Illumination," which was the official name by which the Christian doctrine was known in China at that time. The name may have been accidental, but the inference is warranted that Empress Komyo became a Christian and accepted the title as a profession of her faith. She is described by Japanese authors as a great saint and as one who even had the power to perform miracles of healing. Under the influence of Rimitsu she may have become a Christian and have learned of him the art of medical skill in so far as this was developed at that time.

With these few remarks we must dismiss the unknown missionary and physician Rimitsu. If he could establish himself at the court of the emperor and win the empress to the Christian faith, he must have been an aggressive, influential and capable missionary. He also must have braved hardships, endured trials, met with rebuffs, toiled where there was no hope, and yet have triumphed in the end.

Often the wish becomes the father of the belief. It may be so in this case. But let us hope that Christianity did reach Japan in the eighth century.

5

Francis Xavier, Pioneer Missionary to Japan

(1506 - 1552)

(Went to Japan in 1549)

Francis Xavier is the founder and pioneer of modern Roman Catholic missions to the heathen and therefore deserves a place in our series of brief biographical outlines.

Francis Xavier was born on April 7, 1506, at the castle of Xavier, near Pamplona, about 195 miles northeast of Madrid, the capital of Spain. He finished his short life on December 2, 1552, on St. John's Island, better known as San-Chan, or Chang-Chuang, the Chinese forms of the name of the island.

As Ignatius Loyola, the founder of the Jesuit order, so also Xavier was of aristocratic lineage, his family being one renowned and honored in the history of Navarre. But already early in his life he chose the career of Church service, and so in due time we find him busy at the University of Paris where he prepared himself for work in the Church.

While doing so he met a most remarkable compatriot, Ignatius Loyola, who in a short time brought him entirely under his personal influence. The result was that Francis Xavier was one of the volunteers who on August 15, 1534, bound themselves by a vow at Montmartre, thus forming the nucleus of the subsequent Society of Jesus.

The first objective of the newly-founded society was to bring the Gospel to the Mohammedans, and, if possible, to Christianize the inhabitants of Palestine. But when that objective could not be achieved, the members of the Society turned partly to the defense of the Catholic faith by educational and literary work and partly to the spread of the faith through mission work in foreign countries.

Francis Xavier was assigned, as his particular field, to mission work among the heathen, and since King John III of Portugal at that time desired Jesuit missionaries for the East Indies, Xavier was ordered to go there.

From August, 1541, till March, 1542, he remained in Mozambique, Africa. He reached Goa, the capital of Portuguese colony, in India, on May, 1542.

In India he first tried to win the Paravas, the pearl-fishers along the southern portion of the east coast of Hindustan, but his success was so slight that he went to Travancore, where he baptized thousands and even endeavored to win the ruler for the Christian faith. Eager to convert many souls, he also visited Ceylon, where he preached and baptized many converts.

In 1545 he turned eastward and planned a missionary journey to Makassar, on the island of Celebes. Having arrived in Malacca in October of that year, he waited three months in vain for a ship that would take him to Celebes.

When the ship did not come, he gave up the goal of his voyage and went to the Amboina and other of the Molucca Islands, after which he returned to India, in January, 1548. Here he spent fifteen busy months in missionary endeavor, undertaking extensive journeys and taking part in administrative work.

His mission work was seriously impeded by the ungodly life and conduct of the Portuguese in India, and so, not meeting with the success which he desired, he left Goa on April 15, 1549, to return to the unknown Far East.

For some time he remained in Malacca; then he visited Canton, China, and on August, 1549, he reached Japan, where he landed at Kagoshima, the chief port of the province of Satsuma, on the island of Kyushu.

Here he was received in a friendly manner and was permitted to preach, but since he did not learn the language of the land, he had to limit his work to reading the translation which had been made of the Catechism, or else make use of an interpreter.

After two years of intensive mission work in Japan, Xavier returned to India, reaching Goa by January, 1552.

But his restless spirit did not permit him to remain here for any length of time. Having inspected the mission work in India, he went to China, where he vainly hoped to establish mission work. He is said to have died with this cry on his lips: "O rock; O rock! When wilt thou open to my Master?" The "rock" was the stone wall of exclusion which forbade missionaries to do service in China. Later the wall was removed and the gate to mission work in China was opened in a marvelous way so that Christians of all professions entered and served there.

Xavier was moved in a strange way to begin mission work in Japan. At Malacca he met a young Japanese who had been exiled from his country because he was a murderer. His accusing conscience left him no peace, and he listened with great interest as Xavier expounded the Catechism to him. His name was Hanjiro, which means "anger," but there was no longer anger in his heart; instead, there was sincere repentance, and when he had been baptized, he guided his master to his home country, where he assisted him in his work, acting as his interpreter and serving him as his active helper.

Xavier is described as walking up and down the country barefooted and carrying only a small box in which he bore the vessels for celebrating the Lord's Supper. Often he was given a warm welcome, but often he was rebuked and rejected by the people. However, no matter how he was received, he always toiled, always preached, always prayed.

His methods of doing mission work were faulty. He was extremely superficial in his work, and baptized people before they knew what baptism really meant. He "made Christians" in such a way that the Roman converts actually were not Christians and knew nothing of the sacred doctrine and the holy life which Christianity involves. In Southern India he baptized thousands of natives, and this same policy he pursued in Japan and other countries in which he labored. Yet his work has left a deep impression on the peoples with whom he came into contact. His glowing zeal, his striking personality, his consecration to the cause which he represented, his rugged sincerity and open hatred of sham, his self-denial and self-discipline, his utter self-renunciation and self-forgetfulness—these and many other striking characteristics have made him worthy of a place in mission history.

Not all credit, of course, belongs to Xavier for the mission success in Japan. He came to Japan accompanied not only by Hanjiro but also by a fellow priest, Cosme de Torres, and a lay brother, who bore the name Juan Fernandez. When he left, he put Cosme de Torres in charge of the established missions. This quiet, faithful, enduring priest guided the mission until his death in 1570. He is said to have baptized 30,000 persons with his own hands. At his death fifty churches had been established and schools and hospitals in great number had been founded. By 1593 the Jesuits had 150 missionaries in the field. Nagasaki became the center of the Christian work, with Franciscans, Dominicans and Augustinians assisting—and often resisting—the Jesuits because of differences in doctrine and policy. In 1612 persecution became so fierce and sustained that Christianity was virtually wiped out in Japan. About 300,000 Japanese Christians were put to death; yet when after two centuries of pagan reign Christian missionaries once more touched Japanese soil, there still were traces of the old faith, and these were men and women who perpetuated the doctrine they had learned from Xavier and his helpers.

One of the ablest assistants of Xavier was Juan Fernandez, who refused to become a priest and preferred to serve the Church as a simple lay brother. He had been a rich silk merchant in Cordoba, Spain, and he brought into his service varied and valuable experiences. Xavier never learned to speak Japanese, but Fernandez soon mastered the language. Xavier always had to rely on interpreters, but his lay helper could speak fluently with the Japanese. Not much is known about this capable man, but he was esteemed highly both by Xavier and de Torres, and the great success of the mission work was due largely to his ability to win people through his pleasing personality and to organize the work which had been begun.

Thus ends the story of Francis Xavier and his helpers in Japan, and of their great and successful mission work which they established there. Had they tried to establish an indigenous church, independent of foreign influence, and had they separated Church and State, religion and politics, so that they would not have offended native sensibilities needlessly, Japan at that early time might have become a Catholic country. Lastly, too, had these early Catholic missionaries grounded the Japanese in the pure Word of God, so that they would have been able properly to distinguish between truth and falsehood, Christianity and paganism, the story, too, might have ended in a different manner.

6

James Curtis Hepburn

(1815 - 1911)

(WENT TO JAPAN IN 1859)

JAMES CURTIS HEPBURN was sent to Japan by the American Presbyterian Board, and for thirty-three years he faithfully and assiduously served the Presbyterian Mission in Japan, working from five o'clock in the morning until ten o'clock at night at his various tasks as physician and surgeon, instructor in medicine and surgery, translator, educator, "friend of beggars and emperors, and conciliator of missionary and merchant."

When he came to Japan in 1859 there was not a hospital in the country. When in 1911 he died in America, at the age of ninety-six, there were more than a thousand hospitals, and Japan was one of the foreign countries most advanced in public hygiene and surgery.

When he was seventy-seven, he withdrew from his work in Japan, not because he had grown tired of it, but because he had become weary in it. The Japan of 1892, when he returned to America, was totally different from the Japan of 1859, when he entered; but it cost him and other workers ceaseless toil, endless self-sacrifice and absolute consecration to the task which he was sent to perform.

His great medical skill, gentle and tactful approach, indefatigable industry, varied employments, good humor and poise won him friends among the educated and illiterate, the rulers at the courts and the beggars in the street. He came and found a poor, ignorant, neglected Japan; he left it a better country, richer and more beautiful because of his presence and labor.

When he arrived in Japan he was registered as physician of the American consulate, and he lived and labored in an ancient heathen temple, which the Dutch consul had rejected as a stable. But that simple workshop became the center of Japan's great medical and hospital system and therefore deserves to be honored as a shrine.

For twelve years, from 1859 to 1871, Dr. Hepburn, with three other great missionaries in Japan, C. M. Williams, afterward bishop of Yedo, S. R. Brown and G. F. Verbeck, almost unaided took care of the Japanese mission field, working great wonders in close harmony and unity of sentiment and aim.

After four years of hard service in Kanagawa, a treaty port, a few miles from the present site of Yokohama, which at that time was only a humble village of a few hovels in the midst of a swamp, Dr. Hepburn moved to the latter city, because it had the promise of growth and expansion. Today Yokohama is a thriving city, as well as a center of cultural and commercial interests, so that the missionary's removal was justified. The old mission compound in Yokohama which Dr. Hepburn occupied in 1862 is still standing and in good condition, though it is no longer used for missionary purposes.

Such is a general overview of the missionary career of this great worker in the Lord's harvest. Now for a few details concerning his life and work.

James Curtis Hepburn was born at Milton, Pennsylvania, on March 13, 1815. He came of sturdy Scotch-Irish stock, a racial group which contributed greatly to the religious, social and economic life in our own country. Reared in a pious home, where family devotions were regularly observed and where the Catechism was not only read but also studied, James later attended Princeton University, from which he graduated in 1832 with the degree of Bachelor of Arts. Having become interested in medicine, he continued his studies at the University of Pennsylvania and in 1836 graduated as a doctor of medicine.

Exceedingly ambitious, and having a fixed goal in mind, he needed no long admonitions to make him pursue his work at school, but already then he devised a plan by which he could do the utmost work with the greatest saving of time and energy. He acquired no vicious student habits but refrained from smoking and drinking and observed with unusual faithfulness definite hours of prayer, privately and together with his fellow students. Thus at the age of twenty-one, strong in body and soul and well prepared for great service, he was ready to take up his lifework.

For four years he practiced medicine in this country, and then, in 1840, he went to China as a medical missionary, which, as he said, offered him the greatest opportunities for useful service in the world.

From 1841 to 1843 he worked at Singapore, on the Malay Peninsula, where he gathered rich experiences in dealing with all manner of heathen people, and where he laid the foundation for his great work in Japan.

In 1843 he was asked to take up work in Amoy, China, where he served both as a physician and a missionary until 1846. The work in the Chinese coast city added to his stature as a doctor and missionary, for here he met people much different from those in Singapore and more closely related to the Japanese.

Having spent six years in foreign mission work, Dr. Hepburn returned to the United States, where, for thirteen years, he resided in New York to regain his health and prepare himself for further service in foreign lands.

In 1859, when the Presbyterians sent missionaries to Japan, Dr. Hepburn, as an experienced missionary, was asked to open up that new field and to assist other missionaries who were to take up work there. He complied gladly and served in Japan from 1859 to 1892. He returned to the United States in 1893 and, a venerable old servant of the Lord, retired from active life when he reached his late seventies.

In 1859 he became a member of the American Geographical Society, since he was always interested in lands and peoples. In 1881, having achieved fame as a Bible translator he joined the American Bible Society. In 1905 he received the unique distinction and decoration of the Order of the Rising Sun, third class, an honor the emperor himself conferred upon him for his valuable medical and missionary services.

When he retired from active missionary service, he had won fame, first of all, as a physician. By his masterful skill he not only dispelled the prevailing prejudice against Christianity but also won the esteem and the confidence of thousands of Japanese people, including the highest rulers.

Dr. Hepburn was also an educator of the first rank, and his services were so highly esteemed by the Japanese government that they tried to lure him from his missionary work by offering exceedingly attractive remuneration. Eventually he founded a medical school in Tokyo, where he taught both medicine and surgery.

In his educational work he was helped greatly by his able wife, who, as a capable teacher, opened a school for girls, which is said to have been Japan's first Western-type school for women. Mrs. Hepburn also taught young men the Western arts and sciences, and some of her students afterward became prominent in public life. She proved herself a fit companion for her great missionary husband, and much of his fame and success he owed to her quiet, unassuming assistance.

The mission cause in Japan was aided greatly by Dr. Hepburn's work as a Bible translator. He was the chief translator of the Holy Scriptures in a small group of extremely able missionaries, which included such eminent men as Drs. Verbeck and Brown. When after sixteen years of hard and incessant labor he, in 1888, had completed the translation of the entire Bible into Japanese, he solemnly presented a copy to the emperor with this now famous dedication: "May this Sacred Book become to the Japanese what it has come to be for the people of the West, a source of life, a messenger of joy and peace, the foundation of a true civilization and of social and political prosperity and greatness."

Finally, Dr. Hepburn distinguished himself also as a lexicographer. From his able pen came his *Japanese-English Dictionary*, which was published at Shanghai, China, in 1867. An abridged edition appeared in 1873. Famous also is his *Bible Dictionary in Japanese*, which was published in Yokohama in 1889. These works were used for many years and greatly aided missionaries striving to master the Japanese language.

Dr. Hepburn prepared also Japanese translations of the Westminster Confession, the Shorter Catechism, the Decalogue, the Lord's Prayer and the Creed. He published also a number of tracts on behalf of his mission work, and, besides, many scholarly articles which appeared in American and Japanese periodicals.

Such was Dr. Hepburn's life and work, a pattern to scores of missionaries who heeded the call to the foreign field of service.

7

James Robbins Brown

(1810 - 1880)

(WENT TO JAPAN IN 1859)

DR. S. R. BROWN was the first appointed missionary
to Japan, and he has left a deep and lasting impression
upon the Japanese people as a pioneer in missionary
education.

He was born at East Windsor, Connecticut, on June 16,
1810. His mother was a famous Christian poet and hymn
writer. She was left an orphan at the age of two, and
in her early life suffered great hardship and even cruel
treatment at the hands of strangers. In 1805 she married
Timothy Brown, who lived first in East Windsor, Connecticut, afterward in Ellington and at last in Monson,
Massachusetts. Her husband was a village mechanic. The
family was poor and her life was burdened with much
care. Despite all this, she read much, studied the Bible
systematically, instructed her children in religion, and
found much time and even money to devote to Christian
mission work. Later she began to write newspaper articles,
tracts, tales, an autobiography and hymns. Her best-known
song, "I love to steal awhile away from every cumbering
care," was written at Ellington when she was burdened

with many domestic worries and great poverty. The tune "Monson," to which the hymn is often sung, was written by her famous son, Samuel Robbins Brown.

A son having so pious and consecrated a mother was bound to become great in the service of the Church, and when on June 20, 1880, he died at Monson, Massachusetts, he had more than satisfied his mother's high expectations for him. Dr. Griffis, his biographer, speaks of him as a "Maker of the New Orient," and adds that scores of famous men in every field—college presidents, editors, pastors, translators, authors and others—were "images of his own life." As a teacher he was an inspiration to hundreds of workers in both Japan and America.

Dr. Brown graduated from Yale University in 1832. From 1835 to 1837 he studied at the Theological School in Columbia, South Carolina, and from 1837 to 1838 at Union Theological Seminary, New York.

Having thus been well prepared for his work as a missionary and educator, in 1838 he went to China where he took charge of a school which had been founded and was maintained by the Morrison Education Society. It was located first at Macao but was moved in 1842 to Hong Kong.

In 1847 Dr. Brown returned to America, bringing with him three Chinese boys whom he wished to have educated in his home country. One of these was Yung Wing, who afterward became head of the Chinese Education Commission.

From 1848 to 1851 Dr. Brown taught at Rome, New York. From 1851 to 1859 he served as pastor of the Dutch Reformed Church and principal of a successful school at Owasco Outlet, near Auburn, New York. In 1851 he was one of the incorporators and first chairmen of the executive committee of Elmira College, the first chartered women's college in America.

In May, 1859, he sailed for Japan as a missionary of the

Dutch Reformed Church, where he first served at Kanagawa, and then from 1863, in Yokohama. In Japan he was again a pioneer in introducing Western education and in assisting with translating the Bible into the Japanese language. Several of his students became prominent in public life.

In 1867 Dr. Brown returned to America and for two years preached at his old church at Owasco Outlet. From 1869 to 1879 he was again in Japan, continuing his educational and translation work. He thus served in China close to ten years and in Japan nearly twenty. The remainder of his more than forty years of service he spent in teaching and preaching in his home country.

Dr. Brown came to Japan immediately after the opening of that country. During the dangerous and difficult period of transition he labored with rare judgment and unfailing zeal for both native and foreign residents.

He wrote many articles on Chinese and Japanese subjects, prepared books for school use, and by means of his facile pen accomplished much on behalf of education. Among his greater works are his *Colloquial Japanese*, which appeared in Shanghai, in 1863, and his *Prendergast's Mastery System Adapted to the Study of Japanese or English*, which was published in Yokohama in 1878.

He lived to see the translation of the New Testament into Japanese, to which he had contributed much of his time, completed before his death and published the same year.

For the people of Japan he showed a deep and lasting love, but still greater was his love for the Holy Bible, which he regarded and taught as the secret and center of the progress of England and America, and which he at all times held before his students as the never-failing source of inspiration and strength.

By his able teaching he aroused so much enthusiasm in the young men of Japan that it was largely through his work that the government decided to send the first Japanese students to study in America and England.

There is no doubt that Samuel Robbins Brown is among the great pioneer missionaries of Japan. Always willing to serve, though sickness often compelled him to return to his native country, and always filled with true Christian love for the people of Japan, he was great both as an educator and as a Bible translator.

But now and then one stops to wonder how much the Church owes to his pious mother, who was so poor that she found it hard to make ends meet, and yet brought her offerings regularly for the support of foreign mission work; who was so talented that she wrote hymns and tales which secured for her a goodly niche in the temple of famous women; and who, lastly, was so pious that she spent much of her time in the study of God's Word. Surely her share in her son's work in Japan must not be overlooked.

8

Channing Moore Williams

(1829 - 1910)

(WENT TO JAPAN IN 1859)

GOD, IN HIS INFINITE WISDOM, so ordains the lives of
men that He places some in stations of prominence, where
their work is widely noticed and where, by His grace, they
can do extraordinary things, as, for example, Paul, the
great theologian and missionary to the Gentiles, whose
epistles elicit our admiration as they enrich us in Christian
knowledge.

Others labor equally hard and faithfully, but in more
obscure places, where the results of their toil are less
noticeable, as, for example, Peter, of whom New Testament
history is relatively silent, though he did great and long
service in the Lord's blessed harvest field.

It is so today, and therefore we must not laud overmuch
the servant who has become prominent, nor condemn
harshly the worker whose fruits have not been conspic-
uous. God makes both mountains and hills, and they all
proclaim His glory.

Bishop Channing Moore Williams belongs to the group
of men whose life and work are indeed noticed in mission
histories, and yet of whom few striking details of labor

and success are recorded in the annals of mission expansion.

Bishop Williams was born at Richmond, Virginia, on July 18, 1829. He died in the same city on December 2, 1910, at the ripe old age of eighty-one.

He was educated at William and Mary College, and in 1853 received the title of Bachelor of Arts. After this he attended the Theological Seminary of Virginia, from which he was graduated in 1855.

A member of the Protestant Episcopal Church, he was made a deacon in 1853 and ordained a priest in 1857.

In the same year he was appointed missionary to China. He left immediately after having been called, and worked diligently and faithfully in China, as a pioneer worker, until the year 1866, thus completing nine years of excellent missionary work in that country.

In 1866 Williams was appointed bishop of China and Japan. This new office took him out of the country temporarily. Since, however, the diocese assigned to him was far too large for successful administration, he later, in 1874, was made bishop of Yedo, as the modern city of Tokyo was then called, and this title has become his permanent designation of honor and respect, even though the name of the city has been changed. From that time he devoted his entire time to his work in Japan.

In 1869 he made his residence in the city of Osaka, and in 1873 in Tokyo, where, in his quiet but efficient way, he served his extensive missionary diocese until the year 1889, when he retired from active work as bishop of Japan leaving the arduous tasks of administration to a younger bishop.

Nevertheless he had become so enamored of his work in Japan that for a number of years he served as a missionary and pastor under his successor, for in spite of his many wearisome travels and his devoted service he continued in good health and remained active in the field until finally old age compelled him to withdraw from the land he loved and to retire to the city in which he was born.

Here he died at the age of eighty-one, greatly honored and highly respected by many friends both at home and abroad.

His life and work were like a huge river which does valuable service to thousands yet is not praised for the blessings it brings.

As the reader will have noticed, all these missionaries whose lives we briefly sketched came to Japan in 1859, when the treaty with the United States compelled Japan to receive foreign residents.

But some came even before that time, and among these was John Liggins, of the Protestant Episcopal Church, who arrived in Japan on May 2, 1859, two months before the term stipulated by the treaty.

John Liggins is one of the many missionaries whose names are mentioned in mission histories but of whom little is said. Still this great and good man deserves more than a mere sentence of recognition.

Liggins preceded his famous colleague Williams by an entire month, but was not granted the opportunity to do long service in Japan.

John Liggins was born in England on May 11, 1829. Later he came to America, where he was educated at the Episcopal Academy in Philadelphia, Pennsylvania, and at the Episcopal Theological Seminary, situated at Alexandria, Virginia.

He was made a deacon in 1855 and ordained a priest in 1857. After having served as curate at the Church of the Ascension, New York City, he was appointed to China as one of the pioneer missionaries of his church, and left soon afterward.

In China he served till 1859, when he was ordered to go to Japan, since that country was then being opened to the Gospel. He was the first American missionary to arrive in Japan and remained there for a year. In 1860, however, his impaired health compelled him to return to America, though at that time he was only thirty-one.

Unable to serve the cause of foreign missions directly, he now devoted himself to ceaseless writing in the interest of theology and mission work. In 1860 appeared his helpful work *One Thousand Phrases in English and Japanese.* His widely-read *Missionary Gallery* was published in 1870 and aroused much mission interest in our country. In the same year appeared also his fine *Oriental Picture Gallery.* Among his numerous works, all of which were received graciously, his *The Great Value and Success of Foreign Missions,* which was published in 1889, is outstanding even to this day. Omitting other works of his, we may conclude this sketch by saying that from 1862 to 1900 John Liggins was a regular contributor to *The Spirit of Missions,* a missionary periodical, and since 1885, to the *American Church Sunday School Magazine.*

The influences of his many writings were strong and lasting, and the good which they accomplished can be measured only by Him who so wonderfully and wisely ordained the course of his life.

It is easy for us today to ponder the life and work of these noble pioneers who came to Japan at that early time, but we cannot visualize the great and many difficulties which they encountered.

The political intrigues of the Romanist workers had created and left a deep-seated hatred of Christianity, so that in every village and city there were anti-Christian laws and edicts which warned the people against Christian missionaries.

In his fine book *The Progress of World-Wide Missions,* Dr. R. H. Glover tells of a Japanese edict, posted as late as the year 1868, which read: "The wicked sect called Christian is strictly prohibited. Suspected persons are to be reported to the respected officials, and rewards will be given" (p. 162).

This reads like a Roman edict of the three hundred persecution years in that great but viciously pagan empire, and illustrates graphically the hard road which missionaries and their converts had to travel. Only in 1873 were the edicts removed, but it was not until 1884 that greater religious toleration was secured.

Again, the treaties between Japan and the foreign countries permitted missionaries to live only in the small "concessions" of a few open ports. Hence they could not travel in the interior and preach there. It was not until 1899 that these severe restrictions were abrogated.

Lastly, the profligate life which a large number of Western visitors lived in Japan gave endless offense to decent, honorable Japanese citizens. The West brought to Japan not only the Gospel but, alas, also immorality, drunkenness, murder, gambling, bribery, divorce, greed and other shameful vices, and since those guilty of such evils were regarded by the natives as Christians, the entire cause of Christianity was brought into disfavor and contempt.

Earnestly Paul writes to the Romans, "The name of God is blasphemed among the Gentiles through you" (Rom. 2:24). Let those who thus offend the heathen and cast a stumbling block into their way recall what our Lord says, "Woe unto the world because of offences! For it must needs be that offences come; but woe to that man by whom the offence cometh!" (Matt. 18:7).

Fortunately, the influence of the Word of God was strong even in Japan, and the Lord's elect were gathered in by many able missionaries.

9

Guido Herman Fridolin Verbeck

(1830 - 1898)

(Went to Japan in 1859)

Among all the great pioneer missionaries of Japan, none left a greater impression upon the people or exerted a wider influence among low and exalted, poor and rich, than did Guido Verbeck.

Verbeck, or, as the name was spelled originally, Verbeek, was born at Zeist, Holland, about five miles east of the city of Utrecht, on January 23, 1830. He died at Tokyo, Japan, on March 10, 1898, having served this country for almost forty years without interruption. He had become so Japanese in speech and thought and so devoted to the country that he received, for his merits, the high decoration of the Order of the Rising Sun; he was also granted, for his protection as a "citizen without a country," a special Japanese passport, which never before or after was given to a foreigner; when he died he was given a solemn state funeral. High honors indeed! His remains rest in Tokyo, and his grave is marked by a beautiful monument erected by grateful Japanese friends. Belonging to three countries, he nevertheless was citizen of none.

Unceasing work cut his life short, for he died when

he was only sixty-eight, a relatively early age when compared to that of other missionaries in Japan.

Verbeck's father had come to Holland from Germany, and he and many of his relatives were Lutherans. But because there was no Lutheran church in Zeist, Guido and his younger brother were confirmed in the Moravian Church, while his other brothers and sisters (there were eight children in the family) were sent in due time to their uncle, a Lutheran minister in Amsterdam, to be instructed and confirmed. In the Moravian Church young Guido early imbibed an intense, ardent missionary spirit.

Perhaps there is no other denomination quite so mission-minded as is that of the Moravian Brethren, or, as it is also known, the *Unitas Fratrum*, the Unity of Brethren. At Zeist, Guido met Moravian missionaries who had served in such faraway countries as Labrador, Greenland, the West Indies and many others. But it was the energetic, enthusiastic Guetzlaff of China, who inspired him above all. This truly great and good man served always well, though not always wisely.

As soon as Guido and his brother were old enough, they attended the Moravian Institute, where they learned Dutch, German and French, besides such other secular branches as were taught. The school had achieved such fame that many English children were in attendance, and from them young Guido learned also this valuable language.

The spirit of the school was distinctively pious, yet young Guido was never pietistic. From his early days he was rather cosmopolitan in his social outlook, and being scholarly, he studied the literature, geography, history, economic status and the like, of Germany, Holland, France, England and especially America, in which he was deeply interested.

In 1848 Guido graduated from the Moravian Institute at Zeist and went to Utrecht, where he studied engineering at the Polytechnic Institute, a school famous at that time.

In order to gain practical experience, he worked for a while in the foundry of Zeist, where he was not only skillful but also introduced improvements in the machinery used there.

But by this time he had decided to emigrate to America, the country about which he had read everything available. So in 1852, at the age of twenty-two, he went to America, where for a while he was employed in a foundry and learned all he could about engineering.

However, in God's plan of human guidance Verbeck was to perform work more important than that of an engineer. Suddenly, though he led a temperate life, he became seriously ill and faced the eventuality of an early death. In his deep, inner spiritual conflict he now dedicated himself to the work of a Christian missionary, a work near and dear to him as a Moravian.

To prepare himself for his work, he, having regained his health, in 1856 attended Auburn Theological Seminary, from which he was graduated in 1859 as an honor student distinguished both for scholarly attainments and a pious Christian life.

He was ordained as a Christian minister by the presbytery of Cayuga, New York, on March 22, 1859, and was received on the following day as a member of the Dutch Reformed classis of Cayuga. Since the denomination by which he was sent out at that time dropped the term "Dutch," he is usually said to have been sent to Japan by the "Reformed Church of America," the official name of the denomination which he joined.

On April 18, 1859, he married, and on May 7, 1859, he left New York for Japan. He and his young bride reached the harbor of Nagasaki on November 7, 1859, his first center of missionary activity.

A keen student of languages, he spoke Dutch, German, French and English fluently, and had no trouble adding Japanese to his store of languages, though at first he complained of the difficulty which this new and strange tongue presented. In the course of time he became so proficient in the use of Japanese that natives often doubted that he was born outside Japan. He delighted even educated Japanese with his excellent and fluent speech.

It seems that Verbeck excelled in all he did. He was great as an engineer, teacher, linguist, preacher, educator, statesman, missionary, translator, scholar and friend, and great also as a father and husband in his home.

In Japan he identified himself with the Japanese and became a great power in making Japan a modern civilized nation.

His first work in Japan consisted in distributing the Bible, since he was not permitted to preach the Gospel of Christ to the Japanese. For a Japanese to become a Christian meant a swift and cruel death.

In 1862 there was still posted the following edict: "The Christian religion has been prohibited for many years. If anyone is suspected, a report must be made at once." Then the edict announced the "rewards." The informer of a father received 500 pieces of silver; the informer of a brother, 300; the informer of any Christian or catechist, 300; the informer of a family sheltering any Christian, 300; the informer of an entire family, 500.

Yet, only four years later, in 1866, Verbeck baptized his first converts. These were brought to Christ in a wonderful way. In the water of the harbor of Nagasaki they had found a New Testament, which they had read. The study of that Sacred Book led them to ask Verbeck to give them Christian instruction.

Verbeck at that time was already well known, for in 1862 he had become principal and teacher of a school for foreign languages, which was attended by members of the *samurai* class. Here he also taught Western sciences. The young men, awakened by the study of the New Testament, appealed to him for Christian instruction, and having received it, they were baptized. The converts needed great courage and love for the truth to do this in the face of the prevailing edicts.

Since Verbeck was an able teacher and leader, his school soon became famous, and in 1869 he was summoned by the Japanese government to help it solve its educational problems. Before this, the government had placed him in charge of a school for interpreters. After the revolution, in 1868, many of his students achieved national and even international fame.

When about this time the Imperial University was established at Tokyo, Verbeck was made the head of it, an office which he held for many years. This was a position of honor and responsibility, and gave him great opportunity to mold the minds of men not only intellectually but also religiously.

In 1874, after having served the government for many years in various capacities, he was attached to the Japanese Senate to assist in drawing up a new constitution of the empire. His fine insight and foresight enabled him so to direct affairs that the constitution granted unusual favors to Western educators and missionaries.

From the very time Verbeck came to Japan he had been under the pressure of multifarious and arduous work. He taught and preached both in English and Japanese; he translated books on law and political economy, as well as on international law; he conferred with government officials; he dealt with foreigners and natives; he used every opportunity to benefit the underprivileged and to aid those who desired education. He led a full life in the truest meaning of that term, improving every opportunity for usefulness.

In 1878 his impaired health obliged him to come to America for recuperation, but even his time spent in the United States was made to serve the cause to which he had dedicated himself. Since men and women everywhere were interested in Japan, he lectured and preached on numerous subjects pertaining to his work in that country. He also conferred with mission boards regarding the sending out of candidates and with government officials regarding matters of international importance. Busy always, he simply could not rest, even when he had come home for that purpose. Still, his visit in America was exceedingly beneficial.

In 1879 he returned to Japan to resume his work, and was welcomed back by thousands of friends. He was the trusted counselor of government officials. He translated into Japanese the Code Napoleon, many Western legal documents and treatises on law. He taught at the University and instructed Bible classes. Besides this he preached whenever opportunity was granted him, and owing largely to his tact and kindness, the restrictions against public preaching were greatly modified at this time, when Japanese men and women, under his influence, demanded Christian knowledge.

After his return to Japan, a special opportunity awaited him as theological instructor in the newly-founded Union Theological Seminary in Tokyo. He also taught in a school for nobles, and ever more and more devoted himself to the work of translating the Bible and other Christian books into Japanese.

He was so bent on his sacred task that no one could restrain him. There was so much for him to do that he was constantly working beyond his strength. This terrible strain led to his early death. A light burning too brilliantly, he consumed himself.

On May 16, 1889, he suffered a slight attack of paralysis on his right side, which to him did not seem serious, so he kept on with his work and finally died "in the harness," as he had always wanted to do.

But in 1889, owing to his sickness, he took time out to visit America once more. As he regained his strength, he spoke in both English and Dutch to many Reformed church gatherings throughout the country, bringing them the joyous message of the wonderful works of salvation which God had wrought in Japan.

From America he went to Holland, where he visited the principal cities, speaking in many churches of his beloved fatherland.

By February 23, 1891, he was back in Japan, as we learn from a letter dated at that time: "Here I am at work again, almost as if I had not been away at all—four lectures a week, requiring about six hours of preparation each, and preaching on Sundays. And I can assure you that it is pleasant to have regular work again."

And so Dr. Verbeck went about his tasks. In October, 1897, his physician forbade him to undertake evangelistic tours, which was a great disappointment to him. Two tasks which engaged him toward the end were the preparation of an English address to be made on the occasion of the presentation of the Bible to the emperor, and a formal reply to a number of questions which had been submitted to him on the state of Christianity in Japan.

In the spring of 1898 Dr. Verbeck was having considerable trouble with his heart, but he continued his work and especially also his walks, of which he was fond.

According to his diary, on March 18, 1898, he was to deliver a lecture on personal reminiscences before an appreciative audience. But it was not to be. At noon on March 10, seated in his study chair, he was preparing to eat his light noon meal, his soul was called to give greater service and praise in the home above.

Verbeck of Japan, as he was called almost universally, was dead. Together with S. R. Brown and J. C. Hepburn he formed a famous triumvirate which is held in grateful memory by the Japanese people, for they brought to them not only the knowledge of Western science, but above all, the glory of Christianity.

10

Ivan Kasatkin (Nicolai)

(1835 - 1912)

(Went to Japan in 1861)

AMONG THE GREAT missionaries who labored successfully in Japan we must mention also Ivan Kasatkin,
commonly known by the name Nicolai, which he adopted
when he became a priest in the Russian Orthodox Church.

On the whole, the Russian Orthodox Church has not
produced many great missionaries, for in the course of time
the Church became spiritually and doctrinally ossified and
religiously inactive. The Russian priests usually minister
only to their own parishes, caring little for the large
heathen world. There are, of course, exceptions, as, for
example, the brave missionaries who worked successfully
and faithfully, under extreme difficulties, in the country
of Alaska and the Aleutian Islands, which Russia had
acquired. These few outstanding missionaries were brave
and good men, and among the bravest and best is Ivan
Kasatkin, the Russian missionary apostle to Japan. We
may not agree fully with the doctrines he proclaimed nor
with the policies of his church, but his loyalty to the cause
of missions, his unceasing toil despite the greatest hardships and his absolute consecration to the endeavor to

gather Japanese converts into the Christian fold must elicit our heartiest admiration.

The writer could not find many details concerning Nicolai's life, but the few that are recorded make him worthy of a place among the "great missionaries to the Orient."

After his ordination Ivan Kasatkin, in 1861, came to Hakodate, Japan, to serve as chaplain to the Russian consulate. A young, sturdy and devoted man, he soon became interested in the spiritual condition of the Japanese people, and being a man of deep piety, he soon sought ways to win them for Christ. His evangelizing work was no doubt prompted by the successful mission endeavors of the great missionary Veniaminoff in Alaska, and it is thought by some that this great missionary hero directly advised him to minister to the spiritual needs of the Japanese people.

Be that as it may, at any rate, soon after his arrival in Japan, Nicolai sought to interest Japanese men of prominence in the Christian religion. As yet he was not allowed to preach publicly nor to seek converts by missionary solicitation, but in his capacity as chaplain to the Russian consulate he gradually attracted Japanese persons of influence, and after seven years of conscientious effort, in 1868 he baptized three men whom he had instructed secretly because of the imminent peril of persecution. Even after they had been baptized they did not dare to profess Christ openly, though they quietly worked among their fellow men, speaking to them the Christian truth in love and with much persuasion.

One of the converts, a member of the famous *samurai* and fanatically devoted to his pagan cult, had at first so hated the Russian priest that he resolved to kill him, but by his kindness, humility and Christian conduct in general the young priest gradually gained his respect and confidence. The new convert of noble extraction, named Sawabe, later became a missionary himself and at last was ordained a priest of the Russian Church. In the course of time a Christian community was gathered in the city of Sendai, which boldly professed the Christian faith, after the laws against the Christian religion had been somewhat mitigated.

In 1872 Nicolai transferred his mission to Tokyo, where he taught the Russian language and instructed in the Christian religion those whom he could persuade. After a number of years his mission work was yet more richly blessed.

Kasatkin soon perceived that Christianity in Japan must be spread not by foreigners but by converted natives, so he did all he could to establish an indigenous church, translating the Bible, prayer books and other Christian literature into Japanese. This added greatly to his success.

By 1878 the Christian converts connected with his mission had increased to 5,000. By 1885 there were 10,000, and before the Russo-Japanese War the Christians, won by Nicolai and his helpers, numbered at least twice that number. Though the Russo-Japanese War greatly hindered Kasatkin's missionary endeavors, it could not uproot them, for this great friend of the Japanese wisely withdrew himself from active work, instructed his converts to be loyal to their country, and in every way as children of God to let their light shine before men. Despite the fact that his country was at war with Japan and great difficulties faced him, he remained in the land of his missionary success until the conflict was over, when again he could pursue his work without hindrance.

Nicolai lived until 1912 and so could witness the celebration of the first half-century of the mission which, with much fear and trembling, he had begun in 1861. At this time more than 30,000 Christians were scattered throughout the land, and these proved themselves ardent witnesses to the Gospel of Christ. In 1903 there were active in the mission 144 evangelists, besides many priests and deacons.

Toward the end of his life Nicolai was given for his assistance a suffragan bishop called Sergius, an able and consecrated missionary, who traveled widely, supervised the established Christian congregations and encouraged the spread of the Christian faith in new localities.

After Kasatkin's death the growth of the mission was slower, though the Russo-Japanese church was still very much alive. But now the time of rapid and marked increase was over. By 1940 the membership of the church was little more than 40,000. What remains of Nicolai's Christian church after the Second World War is hard to ascertain. No doubt it suffered the same trials and afflictions which came upon the other Christian churches.

But through the intensive and wisely planned work of this great Russian priest many were brought into the Lord's fold, and the patience, faithfulness and heroism of Nicolai beckons to us today to go and do likewise, witnessing, according to our own conviction and the light given to us for the precious Christ of the nations.

11

John Hyde DeForest

(1844 - 1911)

(Went to Japan in 1874)

AMONG THE GREAT missionaries to Japan we may mention also John Hyde DeForest, whose outstanding talents and long service in the Orient—he served for thirty-seven years—entitle him to a place of distinction in modern Oriental mission history.

John Hyde DeForest had a most interesting and varied career. He was born at Westbrook, Connecticut, on June 25, 1844. He was the fifth of eight children in a country pastor's humble home, and so was trained early in the ministry of mutual helpfulness and cordial co-operation, assisting his busy mother with washing the many soiled clothes of the family and doing other necessary chores around the house. Young John was always willing to learn and always willing to help.

When John was eleven his father accepted a call to the Congregational church at Greenwich, Connecticut. He was a good and faithful pastor, devoted to the Christian truth, which he ardently preached and defended. His mother, a true New England Dorcas, was always ready to serve all people despite her large family and the poverty which prevailed in the parsonage, so that with a warm heart and a kind hand she extended untold ministrations beyond the limits of her own richly blessed household.

Because young John was a bright and ambitious lad, he, after his graduation from the primary school, attended the best colleges of his day, such as Phillips Academy and Yale Divinity School, after which he was ordained in 1871.

By this time he had enjoyed the following enriching experiences: from 1860-1861 he taught school at Bozrahville, Connecticut. From 1861-1862 he studied at Phillips Academy, Andover, Massachusetts. From 1862-1863 he served his country as a soldier in the Twenty-eighth Connecticut Volunteers. From 1863-1864 he taught at Irvington, New York. From 1864-1868 he studied at Yale College, and from 1868-1871 at Yale Divinity School. He was now well prepared for the calling of the holy ministry which he had chosen.

Shortly after Mr. DeForest had been graduated from Yale Divinity School he married Miss Sarah C. Conklin, a fine Christian woman. Unfortunately she was called to her eternal home in 1872 at a time when the young husband was in great need of her spiritual assistance and support.

In 1871 the young pastor accepted a call to the Congregational church at Mount Carmel, Connecticut, a congregation which was in great need of a strong and aggressive pastor. In DeForest its needs were met, for from 1873-1874 there occurred, under his eager and brilliant ministry, a refreshing revival which brought great joy to his heart and spiritual recovery to many in the city. Scenes took place which the congregation had not witnessed for more than a quarter of a century. There were crowded prayer-meetings, special services, mission work in every form and a general spiritual reanimation of the church.

As a result of his successful pastoral work, DeForest,

in 1874, was called to Japan as a missionary of his denomination. He left the same year, after he had found a new companion for his missionary life in Miss Sarah Elizabeth Starr, a most pious and capable Christian woman, who gladly accompanied him to the Orient, a trip which at that time was considered no small venture.

And now followed thirty-seven difficult but richly blessed years, during which he served the cause of missions in various capacities.

He settled first in the city of Osaka, where he threw himself into his evangelistic and educational work with so much ardor that after eight years of incessant toil he suffered a nervous breakdown and had to return to his home country on a well-deserved furlough.

But America no longer held a charm for him, and so in 1883 he returned to his beloved parish, which he now served for three more years. He was enthusiastic about his work and wrote to the divinity students at Yale: "If you should come here to Japan, you would find yourselves in a perpetual revival, the intense excitement and joy of which cannot be surpassed."

He had such great confidence in the preaching of the Gospel throughout Japan that he expressed the hope that by 1900 the entire land would be evangelized and be a part of Christ's kingdom. In this hope he was disappointed, but it shows the enthusiasm of those early Christian missionaries for their work.

In 1886, eager to enlarge his missionary work, he moved to the city of Sendai, where new and greater opportunities offered themselves. He prayed for more workers in the field and again wrote to the divinity students at Yale: "Why don't more of you Yale Seminary men come out and help us strike heavy blows in the empires of the East? If a dozen of your graduating class should come out here, the pressure of the churches at home to fill your places would be unqualified blessing, and the United States would suffer no more loss than when she gave those first men seventy-five years ago."

At Sendai, DeForest began his long career of educational ministry for which he was so remarkably fitted. The city was a strategic center for missionary work in the entire northeastern part of Japan, and DeForest knew that if the Gospel were to be preached widely and successfully, there must be native workers, skilled in evangelistic work.

The school, founded at Sendai, was called *Tokwa*, which means "Eastern Blossom," and it was soon attended by one hundred and forty students. It was DeForest's plan to train so many efficient workers that two of them could be placed in every city and town in Japan to spread in these places the glad news of the Gospel.

The Sendai experiment continued till 1892, when it had to be discontinued for reasons beyond the missionary's control.

But DeForest, on whom, in 1889, for recognized merits in his field, Yale University had bestowed the degree of Doctor of Divinity, lost interest neither in evangelistic nor in educational work, and he devoted the last years of his life to arousing interest in Japanese missionary work by lecturing, writing and personal visits in various parts of the Orient.

In 1905 he undertook a very important survey tour in Manchuria to investigate the missionary opportunities in that great and forsaken country.

From 1905 till 1906 he devoted his efforts to famine relief work, since at that time thousands were starving and crying for help.

From 1907 till 1908 he worked in his home country campaigning on behalf of American friendship with Japan. As a result he was decorated with the Fourth Order of the Rising Sun, a distinction bestowed rarely on foreigners in Japan and one which recognizes outstanding service on that country's behalf.

In 1909 DeForest visited China and was active in superintending and implementing missionary work in that vast country. This was followed in 1910 by a tour to Korea, which had been opened to Christian missions and was responding excellently. From this trip he returned ill and weary. His incessant activity had caused a heart ailment which grew worse as time passed.

In the spring of 1911 he seemed to convalesce, but this was followed by a relapse from which he never recovered. He died peacefully on May 8, 1911.

There are two things that might be said of this undoubtedly great and devoted missionary. In the first place, as Dr. DeForest in the course of time realized that many educated Japanese were not ready to accept the Gospel of the crucified Christ in its pure Scriptural form, he often made concessions when concessions should not be made, so that in his wider educational relations he did not always hold fully to the Christian truth. This seems clear from letters he wrote and from addresses he made, and this can never be condoned by confessing Christians, for in this he plainly erred.

Nevertheless, as one reads the story of DeForest's life and contemplates how deeply he loved Japan and the Japanese people, and sees how he was willing at all times to sacrifice himself and his personal interests that he might accomplish the work which he had chosen, and how lastly, despite all efforts that were made to draw him away from his vocation, he remained true to the missionary cause, then we must without hesitation place him among the great men who have served the Orient well.

Certainly his love for the Japanese people, his faithfulness in remaining at his post throughout his ministry and the genuine joy he found in his work teach us valuable lessons.

12

Robert Samuel Maclay

(1824 - 1907)

(Went to Korea in 1884)

WE SHALL NOW ASK OUR FRIENDS of Christian missions
to accompany us to Korea, or Chosen, the "Land of the
Morning Calm."

There have been so many great missionaries who have
worked in Korea that it is exceedingly difficult to select
from this fine group of worthy men such representatives
as deserve special honor. All the heroic missionaries
who evangelized Korea deserve mention and description.
They were all outstanding, so that it is difficult to choose
from among them a "most outstanding" person. If we
select for our book of sketches Robert Samuel Maclay, it is
largely because he labored faithfully and successfully
not only in Korea but also in China and Japan, so that he
in every sense of the word, is a "great missionary to the
Orient."

This, however, does not mean that we wish to slight others.
There was, for example, the noble Presbyterian physician Horace Newton Allen, who arrived in Korea in Sep-
tember, 1884, and who, after having saved the life of
one of the princes of the royal house, was made court

physician. At his suggestion a government hospital was opened in 1885 which he superintended, until two years later he was made secretary to the Korean legation in Washington, D.C., and still later, secretary of the American legation in Seoul. While in this capacity he served well the needs of those entrusted to him, and his influence upon thousands of Koreans was so great that the cause of Christian missions was greatly aided by him, especially after he had become the American minister to Korea. His work in this one respect was similar to that of the great Livingstone in Africa, who while opening the country to commerce, opened it also to Christian mission work and induced many others to serve this cause in Africa.

But we dare not deviate from our program, and so we shall now briefly consider the fine work of Robert Samuel Maclay.

Robert Samuel Maclay was born at Concord, Pennsylvania, on February 7, 1824, the son of honest Christian Methodist Episcopal parents, whose pious devotion to the cause of missions was bequeathed to their brilliant and devout son.

After having graduated from the primary schools, he was educated at Dickinson College, Carlisle, Pennsylvania, where he displayed so much zeal in his studies and such great piety that he easily outranked his fellow students both in learning and Christian conduct. There were great problems for him to consider, and one of them was how best to dedicate his talents to the service of Christ, whom he so greatly loved.

When he left Dickinson College in 1845, honored with the degree of Bachelor of Arts, which then was not so common as it is now and required much more work than in our day, he dedicated himself fully to the cause of Christian missions as the one vocation in which his talents were needed most and in which he could best serve His Saviour.

He was truly glad when in 1847 he was sent to China, as

a Christian missionary, although the difficulties were extremely great and the hazards to health troubled many missionaries who were sent to that region. But young Maclay never regretfully looked back from the Gospel plow upon which by pious resolution and consecration he had laid his hands.

In China he eagerly took up work in Foochow, where he began a most blessed and successful mission which later was carried on by other missionaries, who succeeded him.

When in 1872 Japan became an inviting mission field, the Methodist Episcopal Church transferred him to that country. Here, as also in China, he took an active part in translating the Bible into the vernacular, beginning, of course, with the New Testament as the most needed part of the Holy Scriptures. As in China, so also in Japan he served as secretary and treasurer of the mission.

Interested in Christian education, he had joined others in 1881 in founding the famous Anglo-Chinese College at Foochow, which sought through Christian education to interest aspiring Chinese in the Christian religion.

He pursued the same method in Japan, where, in 1883, he became one of the founders of the Anglo-Japanese College at Tokyo, an institution of learning which later achieved great fame.

Before that, in 1882, he had established the Philander Smith Biblical Institute at Tokyo, the primary purpose of which was not only to win converts but also to train evangelists for work among their fellow men.

This early mission method was determined by the great difficulties which the Japanese government placed in the way of Christian missionaries whom the people and their government regarded at first both as intruders and enemies of the public safety and peace.

Maclay's final field of missionary labor was Korea, to which he came in 1884 by special permission of the Korean ruler. Here he continued his evangelistic and educational work, though he never put China and Japan out of mind. He thus served as president of the Anglo-Japanese College from 1883 to 1887, and he was dean of the Philander Smith Biblical Institute from 1884 to 1887.

In 1881 he served as delegate from Japan to the Ecumenical Council of the Methodist Episcopal Church at London, and in 1888 he came to New York as delegate to the General Conference of the Methodist Episcopal Church. Both these commissions showed the high respect in which he was held by his fellow workers in the Orient.

During this long period of more than forty years Maclay had quietly but successfully labored in the great mission field of China, Japan and Korea, beginning in 1847 and ending in 1888.

Then failing health prevented him from returning to his beloved mission field. From 1888 he served as dean of the Maclay College of Theology, at San Fernando, California, until 1893, when he withdrew from active life. He was now nearly seventy and deserved the honorable retirement which his feeble health made necessary. He died in 1907, at the ripe age of eighty-three.

Maclay was primarily an educator and by his many literary productions pointed the way for other missionaries who engaged actively in missionary work. His contributions to J. M. Reid's *Missions and Missionary Societies of the Methodist Episcopal Church* on the Japanese mission of his church and to Reid's *Doomed Religions* on Shintoism are worthy of careful study even today by those who contemplate work in the Orient. The former work appeared in 1879 and the latter in 1882.

Other works he wrote were *Life Among the Chinese,* which appeared in 1861, and his *Dictionary of the Chinese Language in the Dialect of Foochow,* written in collaboration with C. D. Baldwin, which appeared in 1871.

Robert Samuel Maclay never played at missionizing. To him mission work was a sacred calling that was to be followed as long as the missionary's strength and health endured. And so he has become a worthy leader of many others.

13

Horace Grant Underwood

(1859 - 1916)

(Went to Korea in 1885)

HORACE GRANT UNDERWOOD was one of the devoted servants of Christ who took up the work of Maclay in Korea and continued it most successfully. He belonged to the pioneer workers who served so well that later the results of this early sowing manifested themselves in remarkable gains.

Missionary Underwood was an Englishman and by religious affiliation a Presbyterian. He came from sturdy English stock, and the home in which he was reared breathed that fine spirit of Christian devotion which characterized so many homes from which great preachers and missionaries have come. Great men in Church and State may come also from homes where Christian influences do not sanctify the hearts, but there is proof in the history of the Church and the State that early godliness, inculcated in the youthful heart, has much to do with the later personal ministry of those who are so blessed.

H. G. Underwood was born in London on July 19, 1859. Later his parents came to the United States, where young

Horace was educated in New York University, from which he graduated in 1881 with the degree of Bachelor of Arts.

There was an earnestness in this studious youth which later at the university manifested itself in his absolute dedication to the Christian ministry.

After he had finished his courses at New York University he entered New Brunswick Theological Seminary, which he left in 1884 with high honors and cordial recommendations for work in the Lord's harvest field.

He was most happy when in 1884 he received a call to the foreign mission field of his church, and so in 1885 we find him in that land of missionary miracles, where God's blessings rested so bountifully upon the labors of His servants. He was sent there by the Presbyterian Board of Foreign Missions.

At first Underwood engaged in evangelistic work, as most of his colleagues did at that time, but soon it became apparent that his many and varied talents equipped him for a sphere far beyond evangelistic enterprises.

In fact, in time he became the leader and adviser of other missionaries in the Korean mission field, and he served Korea as educator, translator of the Scriptures, industrious creator of Christian literature for the Koreans, lexicographer, organizer, evangelist and even as the unofficial adviser of the Korean ruler. Nevertheless, despite all these many and important activities, to the end of his life he remained a humble Christian worker, always ready to help others and ever willing to do his share of the hardest and heaviest work.

In 1909, after having served for nearly a quarter of a century in various kinds of missionary endeavor, he was made principal of the John D. Wells Training School and president of the Korean Religious Tract Society, both of which were situated in Seoul.

Perhaps these two statements mean little to the reader, but they imply that at this time Underwood was acknowledged by his fellow workers as a capable leader of men and as an educator of unusual merit. His work of preaching and writing was, of course, never diminished by his great achievements in the field of education. In fact, as the head of the Korean Religious Tract Society he suggested and outlined to others many helpful books, and he himself wrote a large number of them. But his educational work was conducted on a large scale, and perhaps many of the blessings that came to Korea through him are the result of his zeal in educative endeavors.

Since 1889 Underwood served also as chairman of Bible translators at Seoul, and his influence on the translation of the Holy Scriptures into the Korean tongue was valuable and far reaching.

Greater honors came to him as time passed. One of the honors conferred upon him was a call to the Presbyterian Theological Seminary at Pyeng Yang, where he taught Homiletics, Church Government and Discipline, and other branches of theology.

In 1907 Underwood was Deems Philosophical Lecturer at New York University, which honored her famous son by this appointment.

The theological position of this great and good man always remained conservative, though his educational work brought him into contact with men who at times were ready to surrender some of the truths of traditional Christianity. In spite of his great learning and wide experiences Underwood remained a serious, devoted Christian who was always willing to witness to the glory of Christ's precious Gospel before friend and foe.

He was called to his heavenly home at a relatively early age, for he was only fifty-seven when he died on October 12, 1916. His was a life dedicated to the best interests of Christian mission work, and it was a valuable and precious life.

Among his many books we may note his *English-Korean*

and Korean-English Dictionary, which was published in Yokohama in 1889, his *Korean Grammar*, which appeared in the same year, his *Call of Korea*, 1908, and his most valuable work *Religions of Eastern Asia*, published in 1910, a volume which is still a source of important and accurate information for all who are interested in the great land in which he labored so faithfully.

And so Horace Grant Underwood, by the grace of God, finds his name recorded in the annals of modern missionary history as one who served gladly and well.

14

George Leslie Mackay

(1844 - 1902)

(Went to Formosa in 1872)

OUR READERS MUST HEAR of this great missionary to the Orient who spent twenty-nine successful years as evangelist and missionary on the Island of Formosa, or Taiwan. We speak of heroic George Leslie Mackay.

Let the reader study once more what has been said of Formosa in the historical introduction to our missionary sketches, for there we described briefly the country's size, situation, topography and history.

Missionary work was begun on the island as early as 1590, when the Dutch, who were always interested in undertaking mission work wherever they established colonies, in a humble way began to evangelize the Chinese and some of the natives whom they were able to reach.

The Dutch were followed by the Spaniards, who also tried to win the natives to their faith.

Protestant mission work, as it now exists, was begun on the island in 1865, when the English Presbyterians took over the field in the central and southwestern portions of Formosa. They found the work extremely difficult and made little headway, although they labored hard and faithfully.

92

Attracted by their efforts and aroused by the spiritual needs of the Formosan people, about six years later the Canadian Presbyterians determined to join in the work. In order not to interfere with their brethren in the southern part of the island, as their field they chose its northern part, which at that time was not served by any other missionary group.

The Canadian Presbyterians, themselves hardy and undismayed, sent to Taiwan as their pioneer missionary the unique but most successful George Leslie Mackay, in whom they placed great confidence and who was willing and ready to undertake the hardships of that challenging mission venture.

Since the details of this great missionary's life would take us too far afield, we refer our readers for particulars to the excellent biography written by Marian Keith and entitled *The Black-Bearded Barbarian: The Life of George Leslie Mackay of Formosa* (New York, Missionary Education Movement, 1912, pp. 10, 307).

Even Mackay was unable to extend his mission work to the interior of the island where the almost savage aborigines defied every effort of the white man to subdue them. Only, as said before, Japanese Christians have been doing missionary work among the Japanese colonies after Taiwan was occupied by Japan. This work, too, was done only along the coast of the island.

Though Mackay did not get into the interior of the island, he nevertheless accomplished much, even though the number of his converts was not remarkably great. Missionary success must not always be determined by numbers.

When Mackay arrived on the island, he sensibly viewed the situation realistically and used the opportunities which presented themselves to him.

He saw at once that there must be founded on the island an indigenous church against which there would be no prejudice as a foreign institution. Such prejudice had greatly hampered the Dutch in their work as also the Spaniards, who approached the natives in such a way as to deter them from accepting Christianity.

Mackay, therefore, began to train native workers who were able to evangelize the islanders in their own way. As a result, converts were soon made among the Chinese of Taiwan and among the aborigines who had partly received Chinese culture.

But he went further than this. Willing to become everything to all to win some for Christ, he, in the highest sense of the term, "went native," that is to say, he married a Chinese wife and thus associated himself socially with those whom he sought to convert to Christianity. By this also he cut off all social ties with the country which had sent him to Taiwan, for the bonds of marriage now bound him to Formosa and its people. He did not mind this, but for Christ's sake endured the ostracism involved in this heroic decision.

Furthermore, Mackay, though he was a scholar and a man of great refinement, ate and lived as the natives did, which meant for him great self-sacrifice and humiliation. All the luxuries to which he was accustomed were thus denied him, and he had to eat the humblest food and wear the lowliest of garments.

Since he permitted his beard to grow, he soon became known as the "Black-Bearded Barbarian," though in reality he was not a barbarian but a person of great tact, kindliness and education. However, in those days, in China and Formosa, foreigners were commonly called "barbarians."

His work on Formosa thus constitutes one of the most thrilling narratives in modern mission history. Mackay possessed a fearless faith in God, and in the fortitude of this faith he defied all dangers and difficulties which were imposed in his way during the early years of his Formosan labors.

He was at first much hated by the natives, and many attempts were made to take his life; but all hostility he repaid by love and kindness, and gradually he endeared himself to his worst enemies by praying for them, helping them in their needs and assisting them in overcoming the many hardships of their coarse, rugged life on an island which was not merciful to its inhabitants.

Above all, Mackay's almost superhuman devotion to the physical and spiritual needs of the people of Formosa won their respect and confidence, and during the nearly thirty years of his ministry on the island, from 1872 to 1901, he lived to see a large and successful work firmly established in about sixty mission stations, which included schools, hospitals and colleges for the training of Christian workers.

Until his untimely end—he died at the age of fifty-eight —he advocated a self-supporting and self-propagating native church. He had no desire for reinforcements from the home church, but trained a large and consecrated number of Formosan pastors, evangelists and teachers for the ministry on the island.

He never regretted this step, for after his death these devoted friends of Christian missions carried on his work efficiently in his own self-sacrificing spirit.

What an inspiration it is to read of such godly men as George Leslie Mackay, men who gave everything for Christ, in order that His kingdom might be established in areas of the crudest paganism and the deepest darkness of spiritual ignorance!

May also George Leslie Mackay, the apostle to Formosa, inspire us to give our prayers, talents, our time, and above all, ourselves, heroically to Christ in His great and glorious ministry.

15

Joseph Hardy Neesima

(1843 - 1890)

LET US NOW BECOME ACQUAINTED with a few of the many converts whom the brave missionaries and others that we have mentioned won for the work in Christ's kingdom. The first is Joseph Hardy Neesima.

Joseph Hardy Neesima was born on February 14, 1843, at Yedo, as the city of Tokyo was then called. His native name was not Joseph Hardy Neesima but Neesima Shimeta. Neesima was the family name, and Shimeta was an expression of joy and appreciation at the birth of the first male born into the family.

But strange things happened in Neesima's life. He was led by God to go to America to learn American ways, a great departure from traditional Japanese custom. When aboard the vessel bound for America he told the captain that his name was Neesima Shimeta, whereupon the rough and ready captain replied, "I'll call you Joe." And "Joe" he was called, first as a term of reproach and later a mark of honor and distinction. Neesima, however, expanded the name to "Joseph," since his life had much in common with that of Joseph of the Old Testament.

In America he came to Boston and there met a Christian benefactor named Alphaeus Hardy. The name of his benefactor he gratefully adopted, so that the simple but grand Christian leader of Japan rescued from historical oblivion this fine Christian gentleman of Boston who had so kindly befriended him.

Neesima came from a proud Japanese family which belonged to the *samurai*. His father was secretary to his prince or ruler. His mother was kindhearted, willing to help anyone in need. Since his father served the ruler as secretary, Shimeta was born in a palace and grew to be a devout worshiper of Shinto. When Commodore Perry came to Japan in 1853 and Shimeta saw the strange Western men, he decided that he must see the world outside Japan.

According to Japanese standards he received an excellent education, learning those things which young men of nobility in Japan had to know. At the age of fourteen he devoted himself ardently to the study of the Chinese classics and learned by heart as much as he could.

Soon there was offered to Neesima the rare opportunity of studying the Dutch language and this aroused in him the desire to see America and become acquainted with the ways of people who were not Japanese. For the present, however, his master appointed him to serve as a teacher in his Chinese school. However, other honors came to him, the prince appointing him to be a scribe at his court.

Young Shimeta was thus well on the way to political and social success, though he was primarily a scholar who loved books and book learning. He, therefore, attended, somewhat later, the Shogun naval school at Tokyo, where he studied mathematics and the theory of navigation.

But his desire to see the Western world grew stronger from year to year.

By this time he had read Japanese or Chinese editions of many western books, such as *Robinson Crusoe*, a *Geography of the United States*, a brief *Church History*, a work on apologetics, *Evidences of Christianity* and many others,

for he was a voracious reader and he longed to see America.
But it was dangerous for him to leave the country without the permission of his prince. Nevertheless, when in 1864 he was allowed by his master to make a journey to Hakodate and he was there offered an opportunity to sail for America, he eagerly seized the opportunity and after a long and stormy voyage he landed in Boston in August of that year.

When the ship stopped at Hong Kong, eager "Joe," as he was now called, sold his little *samurai* sword and bought a Chinese New Testament, which he studied diligently on the trip. It soon became clear to him that God was guiding him, for not only was the captain unusually gracious to him but also in Boston he soon found true and helpful friends in Mr. and Mrs. Alphaeus Hardy, who assisted him in becoming a learned Western scholar and a lover of the cause of Christian missions.

Neesima studied at Phillips Academy, Andover, at Amherst College, from which school he was graduated in 1870, and at Andover Theological Seminary, from which he graduated in 1874.

Neesima now wanted to return to Japan and bring to his countrymen the great message of Christ which he had learned in America, but how could he return to his country, when he had to go back as a criminal who had broken a most important law?

God saw to it that Neesima could return. In 1872 the Japanese embassy desperately needed an interpreter and there could be found no better fitted man for their work than Joseph Hardy Neesima, so he was engaged to translate letters for the embassy and thus was officially absolved from the transgression which he had committed.

In 1874, after his graduation from Andover Theological Seminary, he was called to Japan as a missionary and solemnly ordained at the Mount Vernon Church in Boston. On October 9, 1874, the American Board commissioned him to go to Japan as their missionary. He had been away from Japan for ten years, and during this time he had become a serious and thorough Christian.

Neesima was the first ordained evangelist of the Japanese race to take up Christian mission work in Japan. There he immediately began to preach Christ, and with much success, for soon his own father was baptized and joined the Christian Church at the age of sixty-nine.

Neesima's startling career as a Christian missionary, writer and educator in his native country was not to be a long term of service, for his ceaseless work gradually consumed his vitality, and he died on January 23, 1890, at the early age of forty-eight. It is reported that the last words he spoke before he died were: "Peace . . . Joy . . . Heaven."

Perhaps the greatest task which Neesima accomplished in Japan was the founding of the great national university known as *Doshisha,* a name that means "one counsel." This great institution, attended by thousands of Japanese young men, grew out of Neesima's humble work which he began in 1875 at Kyoto, where he opened a college that was at first attended by only eight students but soon became successful.

Gradually sums of money were donated to the institution, and in 1884, needing even greater funds, Neesima appealed to the Christians in America to endow the college in such a way that it could be raised from the status of a college to that of a university.

The response to his appeal was at once hearty and liberal. Thousands of dollars were given him by Christians and non-Christians, for by that time, interest in Western education had become great.

On January 2, 1876, the Lord's Supper was celebrated for the first time in Kyoto. The next day Neesima married a Christian convert, Miss Yamamoto Yaye, a former teacher in the government school for girls in Kyoto, who had been discharged when she openly professed Christ. She proved herself a helpful companion of the great missionary and educator, whose life was enriched by the Gospel of Christ, just as he enriched many at home and abroad by its sweet message of salvation.

16

Asahiro Muramatsu

GOD WORKS IN MYSTERIOUS WAYS His wonders to perform.
Saul, the fierce enemy of Christ, became Paul, the great
apostle of the New Testament. Paul's conversion was a
miracle of divine grace. But are there not also miracles
of divine grace in modern mission history?

Consider Asahiro Muramatsu, for example. Here was a
thief and a robber, but in his later years, when he had become a Christian, he earned for himself by his kindness
toward prisoners a title of honor, the "Prisoners' Friend."

He was born in Tokyo in 1863 and came from an old
samurai family. His father was employed in the service
of the Shogun, so Muramatsu should have grown to be a
fine young man, serve his country, and die a heathen as
did his father.

He indeed received an excellent education, first from
Buddhist priests and then in a private school where he was
taught the Chinese language. In short, he was prepared to
serve as an official of the State and as an example to others.

Instead, with other boys of the school, he took to
drinking and other evil practices, and so he was eventually
expelled from the school. At seventeen he was financially
and morally bankrupt, unwanted by his family but sought
by the police.

From the age of seventeen until he was thirty-one he led

the life of a criminal. He haunted the lowest dives of Japan's large cities, gambling, robbing. He was apprehended and thrown into prison. Here he learned yet more crime. He was initiated into the trickeries of railway theft, at which he finally became adept. Time and again he was cast into prison, but prison sentences could not change him.

In 1894 he was arrested for the last time, though this time he was guiltless. There were other criminals who, like him, had been put into prison on suspicion.

What were they to do? The wife of one of the prisoners sent her husband a book written in Chinese. It was a remarkable book which told of one innocent man who had been nailed to the cross. A strange book indeed!

Muramatsu alone read that book, first from curiosity, and then because it thrilled him, changed him, inspired him. It told of one whose blood takes away the sins of men. It taught men to pray, "Our Father." Never had Muramatsu read a book like this.

A short time afterward another prisoner was brought in. He had read the Christian Bible and attended Christian services. He was amazed to find a New Testament in the prison and talked to the prisoners of Christ and repentance and salvation by faith. When he was released, he sent Muramatsu a New Testament of his own.

Muramatsu read the New Testament over and over, and by the grace of God through the Divine Word he was converted. He admitted his crimes to the officials, was given a short sentence, and then was released for good. This occurred in 1895. His old sin-loving friends at first tried to draw him into crime once more, but he refused. He wanted to do honest work for an honest and clean living.

To secure employment he made up his mind to go to Osaka. But he missed his train. Again, this was God's wonderful guidance, for while waiting for another train,

Muramatsu attended a Christian service where he heard his first Christian sermon.

After the service he stayed and talked to the pastor, who graciously advised him and with whose aid he secured a job in an orphanage. It was not a good job. It was humble, poorly paid, and there were there many things hard to bear. At last Muramatsu made up his mind to leave.

But then something touched him. The children, he discovered, were knitting him warm woolen socks for Christmas. That changed his mind. He, too, wanted to serve others.

He went to the Salvation Army and took a course in the Officers' School. He graduated in due time as a lieutenant, and a task was assigned to him which he greatly appreciated. He was to minister to released prisoners.

He himself had been a prisoner many times, and he knew what it meant to be a prisoner. He knew the humiliation, the despair, the anguish, the rottenness of it.

For a while he served as a member of the Salvation Army, but in 1897 he began to work independently. He came to America to learn more about ministering to prisoners. He wanted prison reform in Japan, and the lessons he learned in America were most valuable.

He returned to Japan and began to work among prisoners. He urged prison reform everywhere, and his services were noted and appreciated.

In 1912 the government showed its appreciation of his endeavor by canceling his police record. This meant for him a new start in life.

At last he started his own home for released prisoners. It was called the "Friendly Home." Every prisoner in Japan who had been released was welcomed in it, was told about Jesus, and was directed toward a new start in life.

Those cast out by others came to this "Friendly Home."

About one hundred and seventy came each year. Not all were benefited, as many chose to remain in their sin, but the Word was not preached in vain, nor was the work of love in vain which Muramatsu performed.

Here are a few examples. An incendiary became a high official in the Japanese government. Another, who had served eighteen terms in prison, was converted, became a manufacturer and employed forty men. Each day this man conducted worship in his shop for the men whom he employed. He himself has long been a pillar of the Christian Church in Japan.

At various times in his life Muramatsu was honored by the government. In 1928 he was given a life pension. But the finest reward given him was the name of endearment and love, the "Prisoners' Friend."

17

Taichiro Morinaga

THE HEART OF A CHRISTIAN is thrilled and warmed as he reads of the wonderful conversions which have been wrought in heathen lands by the grace of God. They move him to praise God and to dedicate himself anew to the blessed work of God's kingdom people, the winning of souls to Christ.

Taichiro Morinaga became one of the leading manufacturers of Japan, but that is not what interests us as children of God. What interests us above all is that by God's grace Taichiro Morinaga became a leading Christian in Japan.

If you lived in a pagan land, would you be willing to write in letters of gold above your car, in which you were trying to sell cakes after all other efforts to sell them had failed, the precious words "Christ Jesus came into the world to save sinners"? It takes courage to do that. It takes joy in the Lord to do that. It takes faith, dynamic faith, to do that. It takes real Christianity to do that. Taichiro Morinaga did just that, for he wanted to win souls for Christ.

This is the story of Taichiro Morinaga. He was born in 1864, in Japan, of course. While Taichiro was still a child, his father died and the boy had a hard road to travel. If a child in Japan loses his father, humanly speaking he loses virtually everything.

With the death of his father, Taichiro lost his house and land and was obliged to seek support from his not-too-willing relatives. When he was twelve, he had to earn his own livelihood, working wherever opportunity presented itself. He thus served a writing master, a grocer and his uncle, a pottery merchant, who lived in Yokohama.

After four years of hard work the uncle failed in his business and Taichiro, now twenty-four, was asked to take a large shipment of pottery to America and sell it there. This occurred in the year 1888. Taichiro's venture in America was a failure, and since he was now penniless he secured a place as servant in the home of an aged American woman, who treated him kindly and encouraged him against despair.

The unusual kindness of this pious woman (oh, Christians, let us learn always to be kind!) produced a tremendous change in young Taichiro, for it was the first love that was ever bestowed upon him. He made an effort to correct every fault of his and to become a good man, worthy of the dear old lady who had become so good a friend to him.

At this time he came into contact with Christian ministers who tried to convert him, but since he was a Buddhist, and his parents before him had been Buddhists, he regarded it as a great wrong to fall away from the faith of the family. In addition, he had been told that Christianity was a very wicked religion, which the Japanese people must never adopt, since it would injure them disastrously.

Nevertheless, Taichiro gradually overcame his prejudice against Christianity, for the Christian people whom he met were so helpful, unselfish and consecrated to God that, as Taichiro was made to feel, their works witnessed to the goodness of their religion.

Willing at last to "give Christianity a chance," he secured a Christian Bible, which he studied with great zeal, beginning with the New Testament. But the Christian Bible, he found, was full of mysteries which he could not comprehend. Of course, he could understand and appreciate the Sermon on the Mount, the saintly life of Christ, and the splendid precepts of the apostles, but the fundamentals of sin and grace, of repentance and justification, of salvation by grace through faith in Christ —these were repugnant to his natural mind. He was *not* a great sinner, he told himself; nor was it just for God to punish His Son for the sins of the world. In short, the Gospel mystery proved itself foolishness to Taichiro as long as he was not able to discern it spiritually, in other words, before his conversion.

However, there were things in the New Testament that attracted him. There was, for example, the intercessory prayer of Jesus: "Father, forgive them; for they know not what they do." There was, moreover, the wonderful repentance of Peter, the miraculous conversion of Paul, the glorious martyr death of Stephen and his amazing prayer, as he died, "Lord, lay not this sin to their charge." Of such things Taichiro had never heard, and they made a deep impression on him.

Thus through the power of the Holy Spirit by the Divine Word his heart was changed. The Gospel no longer seemed foolishness to him, but he esteemed it as God's power and God's wisdom. He believed in Jesus as his personal Saviour, and in the year 1900, when Taichiro was twenty-six, he was baptized into the Christian faith.

His faith in Christ and his new life now moved him to do that which he regarded as right. He was burdened with a heavy debt, the result of his business failure, and this he now resolved to pay off. He worked at this severe task for six years. Then he set out to learn to produce something which in Japan was unknown and for which, therefore, there was an open market.

So he worked first in a bread bakery, then in a cake bakery, and at last in a candy factory. After he had become proficient in the arts of producing fine bread, cakes and candy, he returned to Japan, where he set up a small business in a little house.

At first success did not come to him, for as he tried to sell his cakes, he found that there was no demand for what he had to sell. But he did not become discouraged, and day by day, supported by prayer, he tried and tried again.

Finally he hit upon the idea of securing a car and driving through the city of Tokyo, offering his wares to those willing to purchase them. Above the car, in golden letters, were these words: "Christ Jesus came into the world to save sinners." As yet he did not find many customers, but gradually the people began to buy, attracted by his modesty, friendliness and the quality of his cakes.

As he dealt with the people, he began to preach Christ to them and soon he found those who were willing to listen to the Gospel. As they heard the Gospel, they also bought cakes, and soon Taichiro had to move into a larger house.

One day the American minister passed this house and attracted by the American cakes, became interested in the man and his work. The minister spoke to his fellow Americans, and soon they bought cake from Taichiro. The customers became more and more interested in his wares, and finally also the imperial household began to purchase cakes from this enterprising, wide-awake Christian gentleman. Finally his wares were sold throughout Japan and even in Korea.

By this time Taichiro had become so absorbed in his ever growing business that he slighted God, for his commercial enterprise occupied all his time. Then his wife died, and in his grief he again turned to God. He joined his Christian brethren and once more dedicated himself to God.

Now he began to preach the Gospel in earnest. By this time he was known throughout the country, and wherever he spoke he found people willing to listen to him. About a million people were connected, directly or indirectly, with his business, and these were among the first to hear his message. How many were won for Christ through his evangelistic work is unknown, but his life proved itself a blessing to many, and as he grew older, his circle of friends continued to grow larger.

In the business world Taichiro was known as the "Chocolate King," for his chocolate candy was his "best seller." He had achieved success, counted thousands as his friends, and was highly esteemed by his own country men and by foreigners.

But whatever worldly endowments he possessed, he regarded these as secondary. The one precious pearl of great price was the salvation which through faith in Christ he had found in God's precious Bible, the Book of truth and life.

He enjoyed talking about his business and discussing ways and means by which to enlarge it, for it was dear to him, but far dearer to him was the cause of Christ's kingdom, and though he lived to be more than seventy, he never wearied of his Father's business, which he regarded as far greater and more important than his own business.

It was by the grace of God that Taichiro was converted and brought into Christ's fold. The Lord's wonderful dealings with him are apparent in his life, but had it not been for that kind Christian lady in America, who befriended

Taichiro when he was obscure and poor and ready to despair, who knows what might have happened as Satan, the world and his own flesh tempted him?

Blessed are all of God's children who by kindly word and kindly deed turn souls to Christ their Saviour.

18

Yun Tchi Ho

IF WE WERE TO WRITE the name of this fine Christian
gentleman from Korea the "Honorable Baron T. H. Yun,
LL.D.," it would sound Western and modern, and our
readers might shake their heads by way of doubt or
disapproval, but that was the name by which he was known
in Western circles, for Yun Tchi Ho was indeed a great
and famous man, he being a distinguished Korean preacher,
teacher and statesman.

Dr. Yun certainly was a remarkable man. By birth he
was an aristocrat. His father was a famous Korean
general and at one time Minister of War in Chosen, so we
can readily understand why his son received an excellent
education and was trained for public service. As a matter
of fact, Yun Tchi Ho later had much to do with the political, social and spiritual development of his people.

He was a man of great vision and heroic enterprise. To
him the Korean people were not to remain the "Hermit
Nation," but was to become one intimately linked with the
peoples of the world, particularly the Western nations.

Since Japan was the first nation which came into contact
with Korea, he went there to study the Japanese language,

111

arts and ideals. He became so skilled in the use of Japanese that in 1883 he served as the interpreter of the first American minister to Korea. This contact with an American proved itself of great help to him.

In 1884, when Baron Yun and his friends were celebrating Korea's adoption of the modern postal system, an attempt was made to take his life and those of the others, for as yet there were many in Korea who were not ready to approve Western civilization.

Many of the celebrants were killed, but fortunately Dr. Yun escaped with his life, finding refuge in the American legation. From there he was secretly sent to Shanghai, China, where he met the famous American missionaries Young J. Allen and A. P. Parker.

Under the supervision of these men, for a number of years he studied English as well as American arts and ideals in the famous Anglo-Chinese College at Shanghai. During this time he was also instructed in the Christian religion, was converted to Christianity, and became a devout Christian and a member of the Methodist Episcopal Church, South. The school had every reason to be proud of its ardent student, for in later life he did much to advance the cause of Christianity in his home country.

In 1890 Dr. Yun visited America, where he studied at Emory College and Vanderbilt University, two schools connected with the church he had joined. At Emory College he met Dr. W. A. Candler, who later became Bishop in his church, visited the mission fields of his denomination in the Orient, and finally persuaded Baron Yun's father to let the son become president of the mission college at Songdo, Korea. Thus God directs wonderfully the ways of those who love Him.

In America, Baron Yun proved himself an industrious scholar, who by his desire to learn, his intelligence, his faith and his spirit of love and gracious fellowship endeared himself to professors and students alike.

At this time Korea was relatively unknown to America, and it was Baron Yun's duty to make a favorable impression on those with whom he came into contact. The young Korean did much to make Korea popular in Christian American circles.

After his graduation Baron Yun returned to China where he taught in the Anglo-Chinese College at Shanghai. Here he met a most gifted young Christian woman of Chinese extraction who became his helper and companion on life's difficult, but blessed way. Also in her life God's ways were plainly manifested, for her mother was the first Bible woman to assist the famous missionary Mrs. J. W. Lambuth. Since in her infancy the little girl had been exposed to die, Mrs. Lambuth received her into her home, reared her and finally trained her for Christian service as a Bible woman. Thus love's kind deed was amply blessed by the Lord.

In 1895 Baron Yun was called back to Korea to superintendent the education of the youth of the country. As Vice-Minister of Education it was his task and privilege to organize the educational system in Chosen under Christian influence.

The position to which he was called was one of high honor and rare privilege, but at once he identified himself with the Christian Church, while he labored diligently for the temporal and spiritual welfare of his fellow Koreans.

Since he was a Southern Methodist, he urged that the church send missionaries to Korea and establish Christian missions and schools wherever opportunity would be given. The request was granted, and in 1896 the first missionary of the Methodist Episcopal Church, South, was established at Seoul. On the following Sunday, Baron Yun preached the sermon of the first regular service, which was held in a room especially prepared for that purpose.

As time passed, Dr. Yun advanced still higher in positions of public service, becoming Secretary to the Imperial

Cabinet and, later, Vice-Minister of State for Foreign Affairs. He also edited the *Korean Independent,* though his life was often in danger because of the envy and hatred of his opponents. In 1905 he retired from public life.

After his withdrawal from public service, Baron Yun again devoted himself to the task of education. At this time Bishop Candler, his former teacher in America, asked him to serve as president of the college at Songdo. Already in America Dr. Yun had dedicated a certain sum of money (to the cause of Christian education in Korea), and he now submitted these funds to Dr. Candler. Bishop Candler desired to invest the money with accrued interest in Christian schooling in Korea, but just at this time Baron Yun's father wanted to retire, which meant that his son was to take over all his business affairs so that he could have complete rest. When, therefore, Dr. Candler approached the father with the request to let the son serve as president of the new college, this meant a great sacrifice for him, for he had to continue his work, though he was far advanced in years. However, not only did the Baron's father grant the request, but he also added a special gift of his own to that of his son. This was increased by other gifts, so that the newly planned Anglo-Korean College at Songdo could be established. As head of this school, Dr. Yun became known throughout the land and through his example and influence many became Christians.

In 1913 Baron Yun was arrested by the Japanese in connection with the so-called "Conspiracy Case." After a long legal battle he was declared innocent. Nevertheless, he was sentenced to penal servitude for five years. In 1915, however, he was solemnly absolved from all guilt by the emperor of Japan and was fully reinstated into all the privileges of Korean citizenship.

While in prison Dr. Yun witnessed to Christ and the Christian religion, so that many of his fellow prisoners were won for Christianity. With childlike faith Baron Yun confessed that also this affliction befell him in order that the cause of the Gospel in his land might be furthered.

After his liberation from prison Baron Yun became president of the Anglo-Korean College for the second time. His sphere of activity was enlarged and his services on behalf of his church were greatly increased. He took part in virtually every major movement undertaken for the furtherance of the Christian Church in Chosen. The entire Church and the nation of Korea esteemed him as a leading and outstanding Christian, an example for good to thousands, and a humble faithful servant in every phase of Christ's varied service.

19

Helen K. Kim

THROUGH HIS BLESSED GOSPEL CALL, Christ gathers into His fold not only men, but also women. Believing and devout women have always been used greatly in Christ's saving ministry.

In the Old Testament we find entire biographies of believing, consecrated women, so that already at that early time, when women did not enjoy the prerogatives of our modern age, they exerted a tremendous influence upon the Church of God. They were home builders; they served as prophets and poets; they gave to Israel great teachers and leaders; and at last our Saviour, God's Son, became also Mary's son according to the flesh. Let no one, therefore, despise the great services which Christian women have performed for the kingdom of God.

We do not have space nor time (nor is this the place) to describe the amazing ministry of Christian women in the New Testament. Without Christian women there would not have been a Timothy, a Luther and a thousand other great leaders who have left the imprint of their service upon generations. In their humble, and perhaps obscure, way, Christian women have always rendered valuable service to Christ, and only eternity in its full glory will show how great their place has been in the ministry of the Christian Church.

Dr. Yun came from Korea. From Korea came also, as a convert of unusual merit and service, a woman who always gave her talents to the Lord in His ministry.

Helen K. Kim was born in Korea in 1899. Her home town was Chemulpo, which for many years was the seaport for Seoul on the Yellow Sea.

As she grew up she attended an elementary school which was conducted at Chemulpo under the auspices of the Methodist Episcopal Church and known as the "Young Wha School." It was a great day of rejoicing when Helen entered the school, for on that day her father and mother and six brothers and sisters were baptized. They became Christians because she went to school; and she went to school because they became Christians.

Little Helen was greatly beloved of her parents. She was the youngest child in the family, and, therefore, in a special sense the "darling" of her father and mother. She was so modest and kind that she was also the beloved of her older brothers and sisters.

Her childhood was extremely happy, and she always remembered the pleasant days when she played with her dolls and dishes as little girls do.

Later, when she was asked to describe her life, she made it emphatic that her case was not so interesting as that of others who were won for Christ, since she had enjoyed the blessings of a Christian home and had thus not suffered as others had. Nevertheless, after all, her life was valuable and interesting.

After Helen had graduated from the Young Wha School, she went to Ewha College in Seoul for advanced schooling, for she was extremely ambitious and wanted to make the most of her life. In 1918 she completed her training in Ewha College as the only member of the graduating class in that year.

There were at that time not many students at Ewha College, but an excellent Christian spirit prevailed among the few who studied there. At Ewha College, Helen grew to be a confessing, devoted Christian, for she was influenced greatly not only by the instruction, but also by the lives of the self-sacrificing missionaries, whose unselfishness and ready helpfulness made a deep impression on her.

After her graduation from Ewha College, Helen was given an opportunity to teach at her Alma Mater. But she was not satisfied with her education. She longed to go to America, that great and good country from which the missionaries came who instructed and guided her. She desired to have a wider vision for greater service.

In 1922 she sailed for America, where she entered Ohio Wesleyan College. Here she studied for two years, graduating from the school in 1924 with the degree of Bachelor of Arts. She continued her studies at Boston University, where in the following year she received her master's degree in philosophy.

She thus had laid a solid foundation for successful teaching in her home country, and now prepared to return to Korea, where she again taught at Ewha College. Here she developed her remarkable talent for leadership. She organized a curriculum suited to the needs of the school and also assisted in establishing a junior college where girls who were unable to take the complete college course could obtain at least a partial education. As dean of the student body she so successfully directed and reorganized the educational system in Seoul that it became a pattern for other schools in the country.

Still, Helen was not satisfied. There was yet more to learn for the moral and temporal good of her country, so in 1928 she went to Denmark, where she studied the famous co-operatives and the popular high schools of that progressive and ambitious country. Since the population of Korea is largely rural, the lessons she learned in Denmark about co-operatives and folk high schools were of great value to her in her educational administration.

But Helen felt that she needed still more education, so in 1930 she entered Columbia University in New York to secure for herself the degree of Doctor of Philosophy.

One may conclude that she was a selfish person, desiring educational advancement and influence, but it must be remembered that whatever she learned she placed humbly and devotedly at the service of her people and country.

At Columbia University she studied, in the main, the subject of rural education in relation to the women of Korea, who had been sorely neglected before Christianity came to Chosen. It was her desire to construct an educational system by which the women could be aided in building better homes, rearing their children more wisely in accordance with Western ideals, and employing themselves with greater success in the reorganization of Korean society under Christian influences.

At Columbia University, Helen was greatly honored, for she was the first Korean student to be given the distinction of Phi Beta Kappa. But even greater honors came to her. She represented Korea time and again at important conventions which took place outside Korea and thus she visited not only America and Europe but also Palestine. She was always active and interested in the development of her people socially, economically and spiritually.

But she did not neglect her first and main work, namely, that of evangelizing her people. Thus in 1920 she took twenty girls from Ewha College on an evangelistic tour during which they witnessed to the Christian religion. As a result of this work, about five hundred souls were won for Christ and His Church.

In 1922 Helen led a summer conference, at which she discussed with about sixty young ladies the development of Korean women through Christian organization. The work she accomplished was of incalculable value.

Helen K. Kim never appeared to be old. Small in

stature and radiant with happiness, she always seemed youthful. Her common sense, deep faith, intense patriotism, unyielding curiosity, tenacity of purpose and almost limitless energy enabled her as dean of Korea's only college for women to achieve rare success as a leader.

As Korea's first great leader of women under the influence of Christianity, Helen K. Kim will long be famous and remembered.

20

Mrs. Nobu Jo

THE GENTLE AND LOVING woman who has become known as Mrs. Nobu Jo was born in Japan about the year 1870.

Early in her life she was brought into contact with Christian missionaries and she had the good fortune to study at the famous Matsuyama Girl's School, where she was instructed in the Christian religion and was baptized.

Some of the missionaries who influenced her to join the Christian Church were Mrs. Cunnison and Dr. J. W. Lambuth, whose preaching made a deep impression on her.

When she was eighteen, Mrs. Nobu Jo went to the city of Kobe, where an uncle of hers was running for a political office. He had the bright and well-educated young lady write political speeches for him, and afterward she dressed as a boy and delivered the speeches in person.

Later she married, but her husband died a year later. However, the young mother had a little son in whom she took great delight.

To support herself and her son she took a position as matron in an orphanage at the small remuneration of sixteen yen a month (a yen in those days was worth from forty to fifty cents in American money).

Soon, however, her work became so dear to her that she did it not for the sake of the money but because it gave

her an opportunity to express her motherly love for the
children in her care.

Soon the orphanage became too small, especially since
some old men and women, utterly destitute, appealed to
Mrs. Nobu Jo for aid. Instead of turning them away,
she had a department added to the building so that they
might receive Christian care.

When the police heard of the fine work she was doing,
they brought to her women and children who were wander-
ing about the streets of Kobe without home or shelter.
Soon she found herself so busy with this rescue work that
she could no longer attend to the needs of the orphanage
as she wanted to do.

Then one day something happened. From faraway America she received the sum of five yen from an American
Christian who had heard of her work through a missionary
who had returned to his home country. This fine Christian
man wanted to do a little to assist her in the splendid task
to which she had devoted herself. To him it was not a large
sum, but to Mrs. Nobu Jo it was an inspiration.

She retired from Kobe for three days to think and pray
about a sudden thought that had come to her. In those
three days of thinking and praying she decided under
God to devote her life to the assistance of the unfortunate
women and girls of whom there were so many in Japan.

Having made up her mind, she at once began to collect
money for the new home which she intended to build.
Up and down the hills of Kobe she walked, seeking funds,
and it was hard for people to resist her appeals.

She showed them a notebook in which she had written
that she was about to establish a home for women and
girls who were in danger either of taking their lives or
of selling their bodies for sin. These women and girls
she desired to teach and train until they were in a position
to earn their own livelihood.

But to this she added an important thought. Since she

was a confessing Christian, she wrote, "I want to teach them new hope through God, who is Love, and salvation through His Son, Jesus Christ."

At one time a rich pagan Japanese offered her more than 20,000 yen if she would omit from her appeal the name "Jesus Christ." But she refused. She was a Christian woman, and her home for unfortunate women and girls was to be a truly Christian home.

In 1916 she rented a house and opened a home for women and girls in trouble. She advertised this new home for the homeless through the police and by means of special posters which were placed at stations and wharves.

Soon she found that there were friends to support this fine, noble enterprise, and these organized the "Kobe Women's Welfare Association." Two years later they had collected enough money to erect a new house which could accommodate twenty women. This was adequate for the present, but a few years later the home had to be enlarged.

In 1926 Mrs. Nobu Jo sold her old property and built, near the Canadian Academy, a large home, which included a women's and girl's department. In this new home the women and girls received special training. They were taught sewing and domestic science and were also prepared for positions as maids in the homes of wealthy Japanese and foreigners.

Mrs. Nobu Jo arranged also a special mothers' department which had ten small apartments each consisting of one room and a small kitchen. Here a mother with children could live and provide for her own loved ones.

There was also a well-equipped kindergarten with accommodations for one hundred and fifty children. This proved itself a great blessing for mothers who worked in factories.

In addition, she arranged for a dormitory where working girls whose salary was too small for a decent living could find a Christian home. Thus the social work of this great and loving Japanese woman became comprehensive indeed.

In the course of time she became well known also through her signboards, which bore this admonition: "Wait a Minute." These signboards were intended to help unfortunate women and girls who contemplated suicide, exceedingly common in Japan, as, alas, also in so-called Christian countries. Mrs. Nobu Jo knew that if she could only speak to these unfortunates she might save many from suicide.

So up went the signboard: "Wait a Minute—God is Love. If you feel that you must take your life, why not come and talk it over with Nobu Jo?" The response to this encouragement was indeed amazing, for not only did those come who intended to take their lives, but also others who needed Christian sympathy. It is reported that more than five thousand girls and women came to Mrs. Nobu Jo after they had read her signs, and many of them were persuaded to accept Christ and in His strength to begin new lives. These signs proved themselves so valuable that other welfare associations also adopted the idea.

Mrs. Nobu Jo's work became so well known that in the course of time the Japanese government supported it. In 1929 the emperor, having already supported her work by smaller sums, donated 3,000 yen toward her institutions. She was then one of sixteen social workers to receive recognition from the Japanese government. Assisted thus in her noble work, she could enlarge it from time to time as the need arose.

Strangers, mistaking her name, have often called her "Noble Jo," a fitting name indeed. She has become well known as a speaker for public welfare. On one occasion she spoke for three hours to an audience of more than a thousand, who remained to hear her until late in the night.

Her denunciations of brothels and all forms of ex-

ploitation of women and girls in the service of sin became
so fierce and damaging that brothel-keepers and other vice-
mongers repeatedly tried to take her life. She was attacked
no less than eighteen times, but continued to speak against
everything that sought to degrade the women and girls
of Japan.

Her work has not been easy. It involved self-denial
and self-sacrifice; it meant daily prayer and daily fighting. But "Noble Jo" of Kobe, Japan, is a fruit of Christ's
blessed Gospel, a beautiful flower planted in the garden
that has flourished where the seed of the Divine Word
was sown.

21

The Story of Sim Ssi

OLD LADY SIM SSI was rather advanced in years when the Christian missionaries came to Korea, and so she did not like the ways and teachings of these strange Western teachers who, after all, had no right to come to her country.

What did they have that the Korean priests, who were instructed in the religious lore of the centuries, did not have? Why should the people listen to new gods when the old ones had always helped them, giving them rain and crops and sunshine and all other good things?

Old Lady Sim Ssi was not without intelligence. On the contrary, in her own way she was worldly-wise and gifted with common sense. She commanded respect, too, and especially the women listened when she spoke to them.

For this there was a special reason. Old Lady Sim Ssi knew the secrets of ancient Korean witchcraft. She could do supernatural things by means of all manner of devices which were known to her alone, but which she had learned from her ancestors. She esteemed this art above everything else, as it secured for her a rather satisfactory income.

She first met the Christian missionaries after the harvest festival. The harvest that season was bountiful, and she had every reason to thank her gods.

But there stood the simple but comfortable home of the missionary couple, and with other women, who had celebrated the feast, she walked into the house to become acquainted with the Western strangers.

The door of the missionaries' home was always open, for the kind foreigners were eager to welcome the natives and move them to have confidence in them. Sim Ssi, nevertheless, was a little shy as she entered the room. Things here were so altogether different from those in Korean homes.

The women were greeted kindly and asked to enter, and then the good missionary's wife placed before them glasses of cool water. This act of hospitality made the visitors feel at home, and now they began to ask a thousand questions concerning the many strange objects in the room.

There were pictures hanging on the wall. One showed the Good Shepherd carrying a lamb on His shoulder while He led His flock.

The wife of the missionary had to explain the picture, and at once she spoke in glowing terms—though her knowledge of the Korean language was still inadequate—of the Saviour who had come from heaven to seek and to save that which is lost.

Sim Ssi could not understand this. Such great love her own gods had never shown. The people had to go to the gods to appease their wrath. The gods would never come to the people unless it was to punish them. Old Lady Sim Ssi shook her head at the story. No, she would never believe it.

There were other pictures, among these, one which showed the Saviour walking on the stormy sea. Ah, that appealed to her. Jesus, too, could do supernatural things as she could. He, therefore, belonged to her craft. Therefore she listened with much interest to the story told by the missionary's wife. As she talked, they drank cool water, for it was hot that day, and Sim Ssi ate tasty sweet cakes which the good foreign woman had baked.

"These missionaries are so smart," one of the women

said as they left the home on the hill. "And their stories are so interesting," added another. "I liked them, too," explained a third. "There is no badness in those stories, only goodness and love," said a fourth as she held a small picture showing Jesus nailed to the Cross. "It is such a wonderful story," she mused. The other women held up their pictures. They were so beautiful.

Old Lady Sim Ssi became angry, though her own heart was touched by the stories she had heard. "Those missionaries," she said petulantly, "are dangerous. They take away from us our religion. They say our gods are nothing. They want us to worship other gods. I don't care what others do, but as for myself I will worship the gods of my fathers. They were good enough for them, and they are good enough for me."

But she could not resist the urge to return with the other women to the kind missionary lady, though she determined to go only to criticize, not to listen. Yes, she liked the music, the singing, the preaching, the love of the missionaries. Gradually all the arguments which she could find against the religion of the missionaries disappeared. She was angry with herself for not being able to reply to the arguments of the missionaries. She did not want to become a Christian, and yet she could not stay away from their services. They were so fascinating.

Many a time she told her women friends she would not go with them to the services on the hill; and yet, after some time, she quietly went, too, for it was impossible for her to remain away. She loved the talks, the singing, the witnesses of those who had been converted.

Perhaps she was wrong, after all! She spent hours thinking . . . thinking . . . Sim Ssi had received pictures from the missionaries. At first she decided to destroy them, but after throwing them on the ground she was sorry, and she picked up the pictures and put them gently away. They were so beautiful, after all.

Time went on, and she continued to attend the services of the missionaries. What the missionaries said was true. Sim Ssi was a sinner—a great sinner. She had never known that she was so great a sinner. She had always treated sin lightly. "Well, sin is something everybody does," she had thought, "and it cannot be helped. It is too bad that men sin, but so it is."

But now the terribleness of sin troubled her. What if the words of the missionaries were true and sin would be punished eternally in hell? Her heart was full of terror. She shuddered as she thought of meeting God in His wrath.

But there was the story of Jesus, so loving, so gracious, so good, the Saviour of the world, the Saviour also of the Korean people. It was such a comforting story, and so true. She believed the story, for something in her heart told her that it was true.

It pained her to ponder how cruelly they had treated Him on the Cross. But, she, too, had nailed Him to the Cross. Her sins had nailed Him to the Cross. But God also had nailed Him to the Cross, so that His blood might wash away her sins. "The blood of Jesus Christ his Son cleanseth us from all sin" (I John 1:7).

It was hard for Sim Ssi to follow the preaching of the missionaries, and yet what they said was true and comforting and blessed. Tears trickled down her cheeks as she surrendered to the pleading voice which she heard in her soul as the missionaries preached the Gospel. Slowly, very slowly, and deliberately she walked to the altar one evening after a sermon, and there she knelt in prayer and confession of her sins and made a firm profession of her faith in Christ.

Many in the audience were surprised when Old Lady Sim Ssi asked for baptism. Some laughed at her. Others came to her and kissed her, welcoming her as a sister in Christ. And Sim Ssi wept and was happy.

Old Lady Sim Ssi now leads a new life. She has burned her old tools of witchcraft. She is kinder than she ever was, and with words of praise she speaks to everyone about Jesus her Saviour. And her changed life speaks louder than her words.

22

Christ's Unknown Soldiers to the Orient

WE KNOW NOT THEIR NAMES; we know not their deeds; we know not their graves. Many died before they could do service; many were called home when they had just begun to labor; many worked for a long time, but the soil was rocky and the harvest not abundant; in sorrow they returned home and were received with shrugs by the mission societies which had sent them out. Unknown they were laid away in the graves, to be forgotten, in the Orient, in England, in America, on the European continent and elsewhere.

But the Lord, whom they wished to serve, knows their deeds and their victories. To Him they are precious whether men count them so or not. They served Him loyally in His great Gospel campaign. Among them were women who rest in unknown graves, true Marthas who died serving Him whom they loved.

Whether they succeeded or whether they failed, the missionaries of Jesus Christ are to us lights that show us the way we should go. The work is not yet done. The Gospel is not yet known to all men. Christ's command is not yet fully carried out. Still He says, "Go!"

May these lives lead us to think. May they urge us to pray and to work for the Lord Jesus Christ and His Gospel while it is day, ere the night comes when no man can work! God speed His message!

Bibliography

AMONG THE BOOKS used by the writer the following have been of greatest use to him and their use is, therefore, gratefully acknowledged.

Aberly, John. *An Outline of Missions.* Philadelphia: Muhlenberg Press, 1945.

Authors Various. *Around the World. Studies and Stories of Presbyterian Foreign Missions.* Wichita: Missionary Press Co., 1912.

Baird, A. L. A. *Daybreak in Korea.* New York: Young People's Missionary Movement of the United States and Canada, 1909.

Creegan, C. C. *Great Missionaries.* New York: Thomas Y. Crowell and Co., 1895.

DeForest, C. B. *The Evolution of a Missionary.* New York: Fleming H. Revell Co., 1914.

Eddy, Sherwood. *Pathfinders of the World Missionary Crusade.* New York: Abingdon-Cokesbury Press, 1945.

Gale, J. S. *Korea in Transition.* New York: Eaton and Mains, 1908.

Glover, R. H. *The Progress of World-Wide Missions.* New York: Harper and Bros., 1939.

Griffis, W. E. *Verbeck of Japan.* Chicago: Student Missionary Campaign Library, 1900.

Latourette, K. S. *Advance Through Storm.* New York: Harper and Bros., 1945.

————*The Great Century.* New York: Harper and Bros., 1944.

————*Missions Tomorrow.* New York: Harper and Bros., 1936

————*A Short History of the Far East.* New York: The Macmillan Co., 1946.

————*The Unquenchable Light.* New York: Harper and Bros., 1940.

Moore, G. F. *History of Religions.* New York: Charles Scribner's Sons, 1916.

Thrift, C. T. *The Romance of the Gospel.* Greensboro: The Piedmont Press, 1934.

Underwood, H. G. *The Call of Korea.* New York: Fleming H. Revell Co., 1908.